THE MENSA GENIUS QUIZ BOOK

THE MENSA GENIUS QUIZ BOOK

Marvin Grosswirth,

Abbie F. Salny,

and the Members of Mensa

ADDISON-WESLEY PUBLISHING COMPANY
Reading, Massachusetts • Menlo Park, California
Don Mills, Ontario • Wokingham, England • Amsterdam
Sydney • Singapore • Tokyo • Madrid
Bogotá • Santiago • San Juan

5/87

ISBN 0-201-05959-2
P-DO-89876

Sixteenth Printing, November 1986

Acknowledgments

Just so you'll know whom to blame, all of the quizzes and data referring to IQ tests and testing in general were supplied by Mensa psychologist Dr. Abbie Salny. The ancillary material was prepared by Mensa public relations officer Marvin Grosswirth (with the exception of the introduction, which is a joint effort, and Isaac Asimov's contribution, of course).

And just so you'll know whom to thank, we want to express our profound gratitude to the hundred or so Mensans who took time off from their Annual Gathering activities to participate in the quizzes. Special thanks go to those who pointed out small inconsistencies (which have been changed), and indicated one totally ambiguous question that has been replaced. Thanks, too, to those Mensans who took the new question for standardization purposes.

Throughout this book, you'll find contributions from Mensa members, all of whom are identified. We are grateful for their efforts, as we are to the many whose responses to our request for input had to be set aside. They were all interesting and useful, but there is just so much space.

Each local group of Mensa is headed by a Local Secretary (many of these terms are holdovers from our British origins) and almost every group publishes its own newsletter. We are indebted to the Local Secretaries and the editors of the newsletters for publicizing the fact that this book was in progress and that we needed information from members on how they polish their intellects.

This book would not have been possible without the cooperation of the American Mensa Committee (Mensa's board of directors) and its chairman, Gabriel Werba. We are also grateful to the small, harried, and overworked staff at the Mensa office, under the guidance of Executive Director Margot Seitelman, for their assistance and cooperation.

Most of all, however, we want to express our

thanks and—at the risk of sounding maudlin—our love to all the members of Mensa—the shy and the brash, the young and young-at-heart, the geniuses and the kooks, the doctors and the janitors, the cops and the felons, the priests and the tycoons, the teachers and the students, the psychologists and the writers (yes, even those!)—all of you who have more than contributed to this book. You have, by your being, and by your being in Mensa, expanded our lives and our horizons.

It is a small recompense, we admit, but we'll try to repay a portion, at least, of our indebtedness: All net royalties from this book go to the Mensa Scholarship Fund. And this book is dedicated to you.

MARVIN GROSSWIRTH

July, 1981 ABBIE F. SALNY

The Fun of Answering

This book contains questions—a large number of all kinds of questions.

If you just sit down and read them one after the other, I don't see how you can possibly enjoy the task. It would be as dull as reading the telephone book and would present you with fewer laughs.

No. The fun comes in trying to answer the questions on your own. The more difficult the question is to answer, the more fun it is, *provided you get the answer in the end.* (And I don't mean in the end of the book.)

In my case, however, I know that if I don't see the answer at once I am not likely to see it at all. I therefore tend to give up quickly. In so doing I know, with

by Isaac Asimov

considerable sadness, that I have deprived myself of enormous quantities of pleasure.

For instance, I once made up a small puzzle that, I am quite confident, would stump almost anybody. It is this: "Name a common English word that contains somewhere in it, at the beginning, end, or middle, the three letters U-F-A in that order."

There is only *one* common English word (with its grammatical variations) that will answer the question. For some reason I have found that people don't get it and are forced to resign.

I asked it of a group numbering about a dozen and eleven of them gave up after five or ten minutes. They had clearly sucked the joy out of the question and were getting the bitter after-pressings of frustration. One person in the group refused to give up and was quite savage in rejecting my offer to answer the question. I had to whisper the answer to each of the other eleven, one at a time. The evening ended with my hold-out still holding out and I forgot about it. That was Friday.

Sunday morning, quite early, the telephone rang. It was my hold-out friend. He said, in a controlled and almost indifferent manner, "The word, Isaac, is 'manufacture.' "

I said, surprised, "Gee, that's right."

And, with an almost unbearably intense surge of triumph, he said, "You thought I wouldn't get it, didn't you?"

He still talks about it to this day.

I am under the impression he spent a sleepless night, a restless day, and then another sleepless night; that he puzzled and worried over that letter combination continually, that he grew drawn and haggard and faced the possibility of a miserable and lingering death through mental indigestion and then, in the end, by gnawing at the bone long enough, he found the answer and, with it, enough joy and ecstasy to make it all worthwhile.

Heavens, how I wish I were like that.

That's the kind of person this book is aimed for. There may be other kinds of joy for those of you who read this book, but surely there can be no pleasure as intense, as long-lasting, and as utterly without adverse side-effects.

What's more, let me introduce you to an allied joy, that of making up questions intended to stump your listeners. You have no idea how sweet it is to hear those magic words, "I give up." And there is the added jumping-up-and-down joy of giving them the answer and watching their faces fall. It's much better than beating them in tennis or handball, and you don't have to raise a sweat to do it.

You already have my U-F-A puzzle. Here's another. What word in the English language changes its pronunciation when it is capitalized? I won't keep you wondering in this case: Try "polish."

Here's one more. The United States contains a number of cities whose names begin with F. Which is the largest? (If you say Filadelphia, you will be shot at sunrise.) The answer is Fort Worth, Texas. If you think you would have got it, try G. I'll let you hang on that one.

Or suppose you spell out the numbers: one, two, three and so on. What is the smallest number that contains the letter "a"? You will spend some time being surprised when it turns out that the smallest number with an "a" in it is 1,000, which is one thousand. I hope you haven't answered 101 in the fallacious belief that that number is one hundred *and* one. Properly, that number is one hundred one.

Well, then, what's the smallest number that contains a "b"? The answer is 1,000,000,000, or one billion. Did you get that, too? Then try "c" and I'll let you hang on that one.

One last puzzle. There are four standard English

words that end in "dous." Two are favorable: "tremendous" and "stupendous." Two are unfavorable and the first of these is "horrendous." What is the other? No, I won't tell you.

If there's anything that heightens the fun of answering, it is the sense of competition that might be involved. In this book, you have a large series of quizzes that were given to (and answered by) a random group of Mensans. These are members of Mensa, an organization of high-IQ individuals. For some mysterious reason I am one of the two Honorary Vice-Presidents.

Compare your score with those achieved by the Mensans and show them up. (Those wise-guys think they're smart, huh?) If you do indeed beat them out, as you may well do, you might consider joining Mensa yourself.

If you fall short a bit, you might be interested in what Marvin Grosswirth has to say on how to boost your genius for puzzles. He is the very epitome of Mensan intelligence and virtue (in my opinion) and he has surveyed Mensa members to learn how they go about sharpening their wits and expanding their mental horizons.

So pass on to the book and have tons and kilotons of joy.

Contents

Are You a Secret Super Brain? (and don't even know it?)

What is the *real* puzzle in this unique book? It may be somewhere beyond what you think you see in the mind-expanding, brain-sizzling, devilishly entertaining questions that fill these pages.

Actually, the real puzzle here lies in finding a clue or two to your own IQ. THE MENSA GENIUS QUIZ BOOK solves that puzzle by pitting you against people with IQs in the top two percent of the general population.

Could you in fact be a super brain?

Carolina Varga Dinicu, a Middle Eastern dancer, is. So are Isaac Asimov, Theodore Bikel, R. Buckminster Fuller, Leslie Charteris (author of "The Saint" mystery stories), Donald Petersen (president of Ford Motor Company), and tens of thousands of other people, from high-school students to carpenters to physicists. Maybe you are, too.

The idea for this book began with the inclination to

make it fun and also simple (as distinguished from easy).

The quizzes here were developed and adapted to measure aptitudes similar to those measured by many IQ tests. The stumpers include *Vocabulary,* which is probably the single best predictor of intelligence; *Analogies*, which measures your ability to see relationships; *Mathemathics, Reasoning, and Logic,* which measure your ability to think logically and use the facts you know; and two sections that are mostly for fun but have considerable value as indicators of intelligence: *Trivia* and *Classics*. *Trivia* questions are a way of judging your store of general information. A lot of reading helps on this one. The *Classics* are problems that have been around for untold years. We included them not only because they're devilish fun at parties, but also to see how many you remember. More important, we included them because even the ones you don't know can be figured out logically through careful reading and a little open-mindedness.

To avoid any gnashing of teeth, we've divided each group of quizzes into two parts: The first part is a kind of practice quiz, called "Warm-Ups," to try at your own speed. When you've finished, mark yourself and see how well you did. (However, there is nothing to prevent you from plunging right in without doing the practice quizzes.)

After the "Warm-Ups," you'll find a short discussion on some of the philosophical aspects of intelligence and intelligence testing, along with what we hope will be useful suggestions, from members of

What Is This Thing Called Mensa?

In 1945, Mr. Roland Berrill and Dr. L. L. Ware, both British barristers, had the notion that it might be an interesting experiment to gather together people of exceptionally high intelligence. Mensa was founded in London that same year, and membership was—and still is—open to anyone who achieves a score on an IQ test that is in the upper two percent of the general population. By 1961, the organization had expanded to several other countries, including the United States. There are now about 70,000 members worldwide, about 48,000 of whom belong to American Mensa.

Mensa is Latin for "table," because the organization was founded as and continues to be a round-table society. The symbol suggest the coming together of equals. Because of its membership requirement, however, Mensa has often been accused of elitism; but in fact it's no more "elite" than any other organization that has a requirement for membership, such as the American Legion, the Daughters of the American Revolution, or the Actors Guild. In America, there are over 120 chapters (called local groups) that engage in a wide variety of activities, from parties and open houses to speakers' meetings and museum trips. At these functions, the notion of elitism is laid to rest. Mensans come from virtually every trade, occupation, business, and profession. "If we're elitist," a national chairman once commented, "we're the most democratic elitist organization that ever existed!"

Mostly, Mensa provides an opportunity for intelligent people to meet and exchange ideas, opinions, prejudices, fears, jokes, recipes, in an atmosphere of unrestrained mindwork. In addition, the organization has a gifted children's program, a scholarship program, the Mensa Educational and Research Foundation, and Mensa Friends, a program that works—with intermittent success—with prison inmates who have high IQs. There's also a national magazine, local group newsletters, and over 200 "SIGs"—special interest groups—for Mensans who want to get together, by mail or in person, to share a common interest.

In a sense, it is difficult to explain Mensa. At its heart, Mensa is more of a *feeling* than anything else. It's not easy to put into words. We just know that we wouldn't want to be without it.

How To Take a Test, Any Test

If you have symptoms of test-anxiety, believe it or not you're in luck. Studies have shown that a small degree of anxiety is helpful. If you go into a test situation calm and completely assured, you probably won't do as well as when you are slightly concerned. On the other hand, too much anxiety slows you down and hampers your thinking.

You'll do better on tests if you try to find out in advance what sort of test you are to take. If it requires factual, multiple choice answers, the best technique is a review of facts. If, on the other hand, the test will include essay questions, you will need to marshal your facts, organize them into a coherent whole, and practice expressing your essays in good English, and in an appropriate sequence.

Also, you should find out how the test is being scored. If it is a multiple choice test, and it is being scored on the basis of number of right answers only, you should most certainly try guessing. Everything is in your favor for guessing in such instances, and your subconscious will frequently have a "hunch" about the right answer. On the other hand, if there is any penalty for wrong answers, your best bet is to do as many as you can of the ones you are absolutely sure about. In this instance, guessing can weaken your score.

Still another variable is whether or not the test is timed. If you are taking a timed test, the smartest thing you can do is to skip over any question that puzzles you. Do only those where you can see the answer immediately. Then, when you finish all of those, go back and do the ones where you have to think briefly, and last of all, do those that take up the most time.

Always remember to review your work. You will often find a careless error that you can correct instantly. You may also find that you have missed an important direction that would penalize you.

And last of all, remember to come to any test fresh, rested, and in a cheerful mood. That alone can add 10 percent to your score.

1

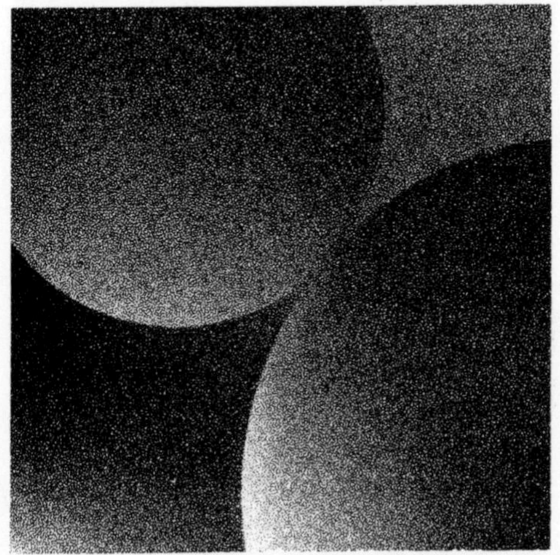

TRIVIA

Warm-Ups

To do well on Trivia, you need a mind that is not only well-furnished, but a little overstuffed. Trivia buffs go around finding new trivia, just to stump other trivia buffs. It does happen to be a favorite pastime of many Mensa members.

1. Domenikos Theotocopoulus is better known as who?
2. Where would you be if your restaurant check was in forints?
3. In the novel by Jules Verne, who went around the world in eighty days?
4. If you heard people talking about ullage and botrytis, what would they be discussing?
5. Queensland, Victoria, and New South Wales are in what country?
6. Which one does not belong: George Sand, George Eliot, George Orwell?

7. What's so unusual about St. Michael's Mount and Mt. St. Michel?
8. Where are the islands of St. Pierre and Miquelon?
9. What were the occupations of the three men in a tub?
10. What is the name of the scale by which earthquakes are usually measured?
11. What species of living things has the greatest life expectancy?
12. What is the easternmost state in the United States?
13. What is the capital of Brazil?
14. What is the derivation of the word "boycott?"
15. Where did the United Nations meet, for almost five years, while the building in Manhattan was being finished?
16. If you commit uxoricide, whom have you killed?
17. Would you care to have your best friend become a lycanthrope? Why or why not?
18. What feast was Good King Wenceslaus celebrating?
19. Hemingway wrote a famous story about Mt. Kilimanjaro. In what country is the mountain located?
20. What's the astronomical name for the constellation usually called the Big Dipper?
21. She's known as Venus in Roman mythology. What was she called in Greece?
22. F. M. De Lesseps is most famous for what?
23. The Strait of Juan de Fuca lies between what two countries?

24. When it is 12 o'clock noon at the meridian in Greenwich, what time is it in New York (standard time for both)?
25. If you crossed Delaware Bay from south to north on the Lewes Ferry, where would you land?

A Question of Relativity

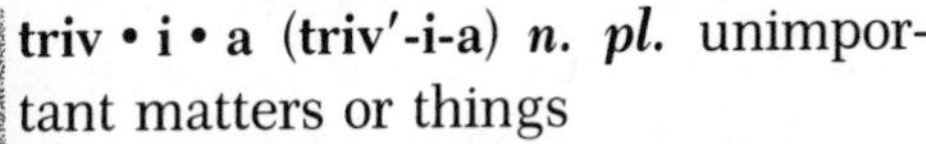

triv • i • a (triv′-i-a) ***n. pl.*** unimportant matters or things

—*Oxford American Dictionary*

If one accepts the dictionary definition of trivia, this question virtually begs to be asked: Why include "unimportant matters or things" in a set of questions designed to provide clues to one's intelligence? The answer is both simple and complex. First, the simple part.

A by-now tedious version of the chicken-and-egg question is whether some people like to take tests because they do well on them or whether they do well on tests because they like to take them. The point is that if you didn't think quizzes of this sort were a pleasure, you wouldn't be holding this book in your hands now (unless, of course, you're the unwilling victim of some tyrannical influence). So first of all, trivia questions are fun. They challenge the memory and probably no other type of question is so capable of evoking nostalgia: for schoolrooms long since cast into oblivion by events or even the wrecker's ball, for books once loved but now nearly forgotten, for youthful voyages and adventures, for past romances and childhood friends and acquaintances. Surely anything that can offer so much sheer joy and a bittersweet memory or two can hardly be regarded as "unimportant."

But whether trivia questions are unimportant *per se* is open to considerable discussion and here, the answer—or, more precisely, the answers—are far from simple. Among the many characteristics that go into defining intelligence is the ability to manipulate facts. This is not to suggest stretching or coloring the truth. It refers, rather, to the ability to examine a quantity of information and arrange the elements in such a way as to arrive at a conclusion, a decision, or a solution. Often, such manipulation is done in a way that we are barely conscious of. It's called *intuition*.

Intuition is not some mystic or mysterious force that belongs in the realm of psychic phenomena. It is real, definable, and, to a greater or lesser extent, present in all of us. Intuition is the accumulation of millions—perhaps even billions or trillions—of tiny, "trivial" bits of information that are stored in the recesses of our memories and that come together in an appropriate combination when the situation calls for it. For example, we have all experienced what current popular jargon calls "vibes." We meet someone for the first time, or even just watch a person enter a room, and instantly we experience a feeling, either positive or negative. When asked what creates that first impression, we are hard-pressed to offer specifics. But that human computer in our brains has received inputs—a facial expression, a mannerism, a way of walking, a style of dressing—and matched them up with past experiences with, and reactions to, those particular types of "trivial" information in the past. A kind of subconscious picture is drawn and in a fraction of a second, that picture is presented to the conscious mind as "good vibes" or "bad vibes."

The longer and more actively one lives, the keener the intuition. There are people who can look at a man dressed in a sport shirt, blazer, and jeans—in other words, a man who looks like a million other men—and declare "He's a cop" or "He's a schoolteacher." "How do you know?" "I don't know how I know; I just know. I can spot 'em a mile away." Invariably, the spotter is right. It is intuition, that enormous personal storehouse of seemingly trivial data.

If the accumulation of facts is so important to intuitive thinking, how much more important is it to conscious, active thinking? To think and behave intelligently requires two basic elements: the ability to accumulate facts—that is, to simply remember them—and the accumulation of facts that are useful. Remembering the fact that in the United States the standard width between railroad tracks is four feet, eight-and-a-half inches is a clear example of the first element, but it will probably prove to be a totally useless piece of information, except in trivia contests. However, that alone suggests the value of trivia quizzes: *They are a good indication of how well you remember; they can also provide an idea of the kinds of facts you remember.*

We are almost compelled, then, to conclude that the dictionary definition of trivia could use a little modification. It would be more accurate to describe trivia as "*relatively* unimportant matters or things." One person's triviality can be another's essentiality.

Consider, for example, the basic matter of the environment in which people think. Among the responses we received as to how Mensa members improve, enhance, or develop their intelligence, there were considerable details about what would seem, on the surface, to be trivialities. George J. Gore, a professor of management at the University of Cincinnati and president of a successful consulting firm, attacks a problem by making notes. "I use a legal-sized yellow pad and *always* a Scripto pencil," he writes, "the kind with thick lead and ready eraser." That may seem trivial to you, but to Professor Gore, they are essential to his thought mechanisms. So is his attitude. "I let myself feel under life-or-death pressure and reflect upon the social value of my undertaking . . . I think of how embarrassing it would be not to find a solution. I fume and seek wildly for alternatives." He writes down anything that comes to mind that could be of possible use to the particular project and then, he says, "with the problem on the front burner, I worry steadily until bedtime." The next morning, "I awaken with a fresh solution . . . I can count on my 'brownies' to solve the 'unsolvable' while I am sound asleep. 'I' do the easy part, i.e., lazy research and fretting." One gets a sense of freneticism, almost panic, in Prof. Gore's problem solving, but there is no doubt that part of his method is involved with seeming trivialities, such as the color of the writing paper and even the brand of pencil he uses.

There are others who would probably recoil in horror from Prof. Gore's method. "Meditation has been such a balancing force in all of my activities that it is nearly too obvious a technique to mention," writes Jeffrey Pickering of Spokane, Washington. "Buddhist meditation has accompanied significant changes in the way my mind/body works," he claims. "I find myself more capable of rote memorization of names and numbers, more insightful, more open to inspiration than I would have thought possible ten years ago." Thus, while Prof. Gore jams his brain with data, some of it at least seemingly trivial, Mr. Pickering clears his mind of irrelevancies to make way for the specific data he wants or needs. Lila M. Mallette, who is also known as Sri Lilananda and is the coordinator of Mensa's Human Potential Special Interest Group (SIG), points out that effective meditation requires attention to such seeming trivialities as the kind of clothing one wears, the room temperature, the amount of light, and even the surface on which one is lying.

If the cramming-the-head process or the total-clearing-of-the-brain process seems unsuited to your own style, you may want to consider an old but no less effective technique for remembering trivia. Irvin

K. Sasaki, a schoolteacher in Honolulu, finds mnemonics (devices that aid the memory) useful in teaching his students. His favorite type "is a sentence made up of the beginning letters of the data to be learned or remembered." It can be a nonsense sentence, of course, and even a humorous one, but the key, according to Mr. Sasaki, is that "one should make up his own sentence around a topic or situation that interests him." By way of example, he relates how he invited a group of fifth-graders to devise a mnemonic that would help them remember the original thirteen American colonies, in order of settlement. Here is what they came up with: "Vicious MonSters Hate Yukky Cooking. ManY Really Dig Papayas 'N' Juicy Sweet Guavas." (Virginia, MasSachusetts, New Hampshire, New York, Connecticut, MarYland, Rhode Island, Delaware, PennsYlvania, North Carolina, New Jersey, South Carolina, Georgia.) "Note," he notes, "the preoccupation of ten- and eleven-year-olds with monsters and, also, the delicious tropical touch that flowed naturally from kids living in Hawaii who have to learn about far-away sister states."

Noted. Also noted is the fact that sometimes the mnemonic is as difficult to remember as the data it is supposed to help you remember. Perhaps, if I were a ten-year-old Hawaiian. . . .

And now, if you are sufficiently impressed with the notion that trivia isn't necessarily trivial, go on to the next section. But don't take it *too* seriously. Just have some fun, and maybe enjoy a few memories.

Match Wits with Mensa

TRIVIA TEST

Time started ____________
Time elapsed ____________

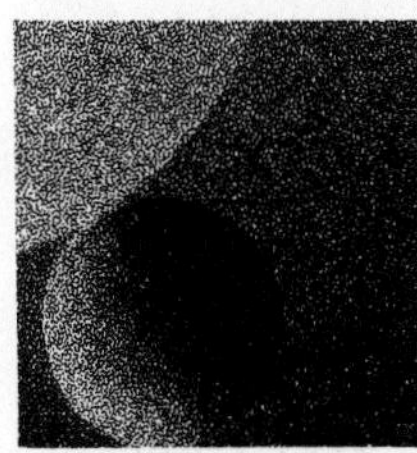

1. François Marie Arouet is better known as who?
2. If Cortez conquered Mexico, who conquered Peru?
3. Your friend gives you some nice Barsac. What do you have?
4. Where is Karl Marx buried?
5. Where would you be if your hotel bill was charged in markka?
6. What do dodo birds and kiwi birds have in common?
7. A distich is a rhyming couplet; what is a tryptich?
8. Which one of the following does not belong? Caravaggio, Corot, Copley, Cellini.

9. What does a dolorimeter measure?
10. If you had triskadekaphobia, what would you be afraid of?
11. Ferdinand and Isabella (of Columbus fame) had a daughter who became Queen of England. Who was her husband?
12. Samuel Clemens is better known as who?
13. What is the river, in mythology, that guards the Underworld?
14. What is the old Roman province of Lusitania called today?
15. Which American politician was known as "The Veep?"
16. Nobel gave funds for the Peace Prize. What did he help to invent or develop?
17. Name two of the Channel Islands that lie between England and France.
18. A new word, "serendipity," was coined from the title of a book, *The Three Princes of Serendip.* Where was Serendip?
19. Nock, fletching, and shaft. What sport uses these?
20. Argent, or, passant, rampant: To what do these terms refer?
21. If you order a restaurant dish that has Florentine in its name, what ingredient should you expect in the dish?
22. Gold is Au, Silver is Ag. What is Platinum?
23. If you went from New York to Rio de Janeiro, in what general direction would you be traveling?

24. To what country does Greenland belong?
25. If you crossed the Kill van Kull from north to south, where would you be?

Time finished ____________

2

VOCABULARY

Warm-Ups

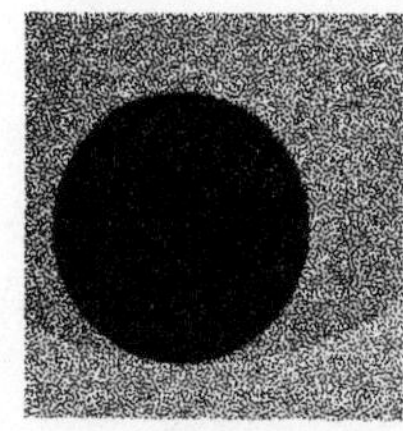

Try to choose the best definition of these words by yourself. Then try the second half—the Vocabulary test, which has been timed and normed against Mensa members. Good luck:

1. Paramount
   a) a range of hills in Paraguay
   b) top of a mountain
   c) above all others, superior
   d) semi-hilly
   e) beyond a particular range of hills
2. Pagan
   a) a variety of farm wagon
   b) a feast of certain Northwest tribes
   c) a form of payment in a barter system
   d) a heathen, one not believing in the true God
   e) an Indian home, round, with a hole in the top
   for smoke

3. Allay
   a) a former spelling of "alley"
   b) a French expression, meaning "Let's go!"
   c) to assuage; to temper or abate
   d) a form of soil, layered in types of earth
   e) a scoring term in hockey
4. Suppliant
   a) extremely limber and lithe
   b) folded in pleats, like a kilt
   c) of surpassing excellence
   d) a humble petitioner
   e) one who does not tell the truth
5. Dynastic
   a) pertaining to an explosive
   b) related to a Chinese type of antique
   c) pertaining to a succession of rulers from the same family or line
   d) pertaining to the state of being active or engaged in some activity
   e) related to the famous Dynas family of history
6. Feudal
   a) relating to antagonism between friends or relatives
   b) pertaining to the land-holding relationship between lord and vassal
   c) a particular type of shield used in heraldry to show historic descent
   d) pertaining to medieval songs and ballads
   e) pertaining to the clan warfare in Scotland in the early middle ages
7. Improvise

a) to be improvident and unthrifty; a spendthrift
b) to speak or perform on the spur of the moment; to act without previous plan
c) to act in a thrifty, forehanded, calculated manner
d) to lay in provisions
e) to require performance of a bond, as in a court of law

8. Metamorphosis
   a) a state of hypnotic sleepiness, medically induced
   b) the action or process of changing in shape or form
   c) a newly developed sleep-inducing drug
   d) a variety of vegetable preservative
   e) an extraordinarily large tropical moth
9. Paroxysm
   a) a fit (often figurative)
   b) a type of hairstyle adopted in Japan
   c) a bout of coughing
   d) an intellectual division between individuals
   e) a rift in a valley
10. Capricious
    a) relating to cooked goat or kid
    b) relating to an astrological sign
    c) unreasonable, arbitrary, stern
    d) fantastic, whimsical
    e) light and full of luminescence
11. Plebian
    a) poor, without money
    b) one of a group of soldiers

c) the electorate
d) one of, or pertaining to, the common people
e) one of, or pertaining to, the elite

12. Iniquity
a) unequal balances and scales in weighing
b) a new type of investment often called a Money Market fund
c) a gross injustice or public wrong; a sin
d) a climate that suffers from extremes of heat or cold
e) a legal term for an uneven distribution of assets in a bankruptcy

13. Pretentious
a) a pretense of someone who holds himself out as an elected officer, for example, or a doctor
b) showy, ostentatious, making claims (especially unwarranted) to great importance
c) a prevarication; a deliberate lie
d) fighting, angry, full of argumentative manners
e) very attentive and careful

14. Extant
a) a nautical measuring instrument
b) in existence, continuting to exist
c) a variety of insect, not found in North America
d) derived from a musical instrument
e) in addition to, above and beyond what is required

15. Perturbed
a) completely reversed in direction
b) pertaining to the building of large edifices
c) related to the inner part of cities

d) greatly agitated, discomposed, disturbed greatly
e) of, or pertaining to, through-traffic patterns

16. Usurp
    a) a style of noisy eating, especially liquids
    b) reverting back to an original state
    c) to appropriate wrongfully, especially for oneself
    d) old form of adjective relating to the U.S.
    e) above and beyond
17. Apparition
    a) a form of chemical instrumentation
    b) a form of biological instrumentation
    c) a ghost, phantom, immaterial object
    d) a camera originally developed to take pictures without film plates
    e) a particular style of clothing design
18. Circumlocution
    a) the surrounding walls of a city
    b) the moat surrounding a castle
    c) a walk around anything, or the outside of something
    d) a roundabout expression; the use of many words for few
    e) a complete trip around the world
19. Staunch
    a) strong, firm, resolute
    b) having a strong odor
    c) pertaining to a tree
    d) in chemistry, a term for noxious vapors
    e) improper, not moral, or ethical
20. Noisome
    a) appallingly loud

b) harmful, bad smelling
c) noisy in a pleasant sense, like music
d) overly generous with praise
e) peculiar, highly eccentric

In a Word . . .

When confronted by a member attempting to explain and describe Mensa, people who have never before heard of it inevitably ask: "But what does Mensa do?" And just as inevitably, the answer comes back: "Well, it's mostly a social organization." This is often followed by a discussion of the need for intelligent people to communicate with each other and to meet people of diverse interests and backgrounds. It's not unusual, at a Mensa function, to find a group comprised of, say, a schoolteacher, a computer programmer, a bank teller, a carpenter, and a nuclear physicist locked in lively conversation. What Mensans do best is talk. Of course, it's not the only thing they do: While Mensa *is* a social organization, it is constitutionally committed to the fostering of human intelligence through various programs. But everything depends on communication. And obviously, the ability to communicate—whether talking, writing, or listening—depends a great deal on the versatility of the communicator. Conversation has been described as an art. That may be overstating the case somewhat, but for our purposes it offers a useful analogy. Let's make a few comparisons.

The ability to paint or draw is a talent—a gift, if you will. Many people believe that intelligence or, more precisely, a high IQ is also a gift. If you give a person with drawing talent a pencil and paper, he or she will draw some very nice pictures, perhaps even some great pictures. Similarly, if a person with a high IQ is given a basic vocabulary, he or she will express some interesting, perhaps even profound, ideas. But give the drawer a variety of media—oils, pastels, water colors, paper, canvas, wood, even a camera and film—and teach their use, and both the artistic output and its quality will be considerably greater. Again, if a person with a high IQ is given a variety of media—words, grammar, punctuation, other languages—he or she will be better able to produce ideas.

Just as an artist with the need for self-expression will somehow manage to acquire the media which are best suited to that expression a person with a high IQ is likely to acquire the words necessary for his or her expression. Thus, we find ourselves in yet another chicken-and-egg dilemma. Most experts agree that a large and well-used vocabulary is an important—perhaps *the* most important—indicator of a high IQ, but do intelligent people naturally add to their store of words, or does the accumulation of words enhance a person's IQ? The answer to both is probably yes. To some extent, at least, intelligence is hereditary, but psychologists and others playing the IQ game tend to agree that environment, which includes both formal and informal education, has a profound effect on intelligence. (If you enjoy lively arguments in which the participants nearly come to blows, try to get two or three academicians to agree on the *extent* to which heredity and environment influence intelligence!)

It should come as no surprise, therefore, that of all the games, quizzes, and puzzles that abound, Mensans prefer those involving words and, as the following quiz indicates, those are the kind in which they do best. Of all the quizzes in this book, Mensans scored highest in this section. At almost every Regional or Annual Gathering you'll find a game room, and almost any time of the day or night, you'll find people there. To be sure, some will be playing bridge, or chess, or backgammon, or Dungeons and Dragons (a widely popular game in Mensa), but they are usually outnumbered by those playing Scrabble®, or Boggle®, or Perquacky®, or anagrams, or any of the other word games that abound. Even when they're alone, Mensans enjoy vocabulary challenges, as evidenced by those who responded to our request for tips and techniques of exercising and strengthening one's intelligence.

One favorite is Dictionary, a game that can be played solo or with others. Its rules are simple: The player simply flips open a reasonably large dictionary at random and the other player (if there is one) must define the first word (or, if you prefer, the last word) that appears on either page. Some people define the first word with more than two syllables. The variations are many, as are the methods of scoring. Feel free to make up your own.

Ed Oram of Atlanta was one of several members who offered an old, reliable technique for vocabulary stretching plus a mind-bending variation: anagrams. "I write a word, say *galleon*," he says, "then list as many words of four or more letters from the parent word, excluding proper names, plurals, and foreign words."

That was as far as I got in Ed's letter. I took another look at *galleon*, and in the margin jotted down *gall, gale, goal, gone, lone, angle, angel, legal, eagle, glen, gaol* (British for "jail"), *loge, ogle,* and *alone*. That took about three minutes and then I got stuck, so I forced myself to get back to work (i.e., writing this book). Why did I time myself? I have no idea; it just seemed the thing to do.

As though his little anagrammatic exercise did not cause enough trouble, Ed added the following:

> Whenever I really want to exercise my mind, I revert to an old problem I invented over twenty years ago, and have not yet solved: to create any 5 × 5 array of the letters of the alphabet (excluding Q), whereby all adjacent letters in the array can be linked by spelling out words:

```
Z – C – M   P – X
  \ |    \  |  /
S   A – R – E   Y
      /     |
W   T – H – G   D
            |
B   O   U   I – L
            |   |
J   F   V   N – K
```

> Draw a line to link the letters in *knight, acme, expert, czar, ilk,* etc. There are 72 such links to be made altogether. My best score to date is 68. The letters may be rearranged at will; for example, in the above square, if R-H and G-D were interchanged, then *fjord* could be spelled out, but then H would be next to M, perhaps causing a problem there, unless O and T were interchanged to get *ohm*, but then J and T would create difficulties. . . .
>
> This problem . . . can be tackled any time a pencil and paper are handy. Doubling of letters (e.g., *three*) or double use (e.g., *hedge*) are permitted . . . I'd love to see a solution to this problem before I die, but usually, F, V, and J are uncooperative. . . .

If you think you can solve the problem, you're certainly welcome to try. Send your solutions to *Mensa Book,* 1701 West Third St., Brooklyn, NY 11223. There are no prizes or awards, except the knowledge that you may help Ed Oram die a happy man.

Many word games and exercises seem silly and boring at first, but to a word lover, they frequently lay insidious traps. Case in point: a little exercise invented by Carlotta Follansbee of The Bronx, NY. "I have devised a game," she wrote, "to while away the time spent in the wrong traffic lane. Many license plates carry three letters. Very often these letters can be used in the same order (though not necessarily next to each other) in an English (or other) word." She then offers the following examples:

WKW – awkward
FCN – confection
JTL – judgmental
ABC – abacus
HHD – shepherd
AEK – gaekwar
HRU – thrust, through

"I try not to use the plural S, or to use I or N or G in *-ing* endings. Since so many New Jersey plates have a J, in my own game I allow myself to use it as a soft G—PJN can be *pigeon,* but not *pigpen*—I also use Q for O."

Nice try, I thought, but it's a boring game. I decided not to include it in this book. A day or two later, my wife, my son, and I were on our way to the neighborhood playground and Carlotta's game came to mind. I decided, in all fairness, to give it a try. That was a mistake: All conversation ceased as I began peering at the license plates of the passing cars, getting more and more hooked on the game. I found that the longer I played it, the more I wanted to play it. *Warning: Carlotta Follansbee's license-plate word game is addictive!*

"Since I am hopeless with languages," she added, almost as an afterthought, "I give myself an extra pat on the back when a combination like ABG yields a word like *abogado,* or when a group like HRU (see above list) provides *uhuru.*" *Gaekwar* isn't bad either, Carlotta. Incidentally, she points out that some children play the game very well. If yours do, it may be an indication of "giftedness"—that is, smart, as opposed to smart-alecky.

You probably already know the simplest time-tested method of increasing your vocabulary and thereby expanding your intelligence, but it's worth mentioning as a reminder: Whenever you come across an unfamiliar word first try to derive its meaning from the context in which it is used. Then write it down and when you get a chance, look it up in the dictionary. Even if the dictionary is at hand and you can look up the word immediately, write it down anyway. Writing it helps to imprint it on your memory. The exception, of course, is in the quiz that follows: If you take the time to look up unfamiliar words, it will play havoc with your timekeeping. Maybe you can put a little pencil mark next to the words you don't know and look them up later, even though they're defined, more or less, in the answers.

All right; you've stalled long enough. It's time to turn to the quiz.

Match Wits with Mensa

VOCABULARY TEST

Time started ____________
Time elapsed ____________

A favorite author of many Mensa members is Isaac Asimov. The following words were taken from some of his books.

1. Conglomeration
   a) a fire
   b) a catastrophe
   c) a clustered mass
   d) a net
   e) a matching
2. Stagnation
   a) deer
   b) a union of countries
   c) absence of activity, usually unhealthy

   d) able to be reduced to lowest possible terms
   e) inflation of monetary currencies

3. Eloquent
   a) omitting one or more words in a sentence, for effect
   b) possessing or exercising the power of fluent, appropriate, expression
   c) flowing smoothly, like a river with considerable current
   d) a building of a particular size and shape
   e) dangerous, because of certain characteristics
4. Sibilant
   a) children having one or both parents in common
   b) a Greek character who could foretell the future
   c) a substance that dries up moisture
   d) having a hissing sound
   e) living in, or being a citizen of, Sibilis
5. Apocryphal
   a) biblical
   b) spurious, mythical, of doubtful authenticity
   c) written anonymously
   d) pertaining to the Antipodes
   e) handwritten
6. Inveigle
   a) to rail against
   b) to dress in veils, as for a dance
   c) to beguile or deceive
   d) invert
   e) to turn into another object, as by magic

7. Sordid
   a) dirty, squalid, mean, despicable
   b) deaf, hard of hearing
   c) a type of acid
   d) a thing of small value, a trifle
   e) a scab
8. Antagonism
   a) a country in Asia Minor
   b) active opposition
   c) a predecessor
   d) an antidote to poison
   e) a flower cluster on a single stem
9. Mountebank
   a) an Alpine banking organization
   b) an Italian flower
   c) a charlatan, a quack
   d) a card game involving cheating
   e) enveloped in a crust
10. Legerdemain
    a) a kind of imported handgun
    b) the Italian name for the town of Leghorn
    c) sleight of hand, conjuring tricks
    d) a former prime minister of France
    e) the title of a famous poem by Keats
11. Implicit
    a) implied, although perhaps not expressed
    b) built-in guarantee
    c) not legal
    d) a medieval household tool
    e) above and beyond the usual

12. Hegemony
    a) a musical mode
    b) a form of Greek poetry
    c) the opposite of entropy
    d) the predominance of one state in a confederacy
    e) the act of analyzing the linguistic structure of words
13. Periphery
    a) outer surface, circumference; a surrounding region or area
    b) traveling widely
    c) a hemispherical shape
    d) a variety of worm-like creatures that inhabit Africa
    e) an angle of more than 90°
14. Solicitous
    a) all alone, without company
    b) anxious, troubled, or deeply concerned
    c) involved with a solicitor or lawyer (especially British)
    d) being perfectly united, or of one opinion, with a group
    e) the theory that involves the study of knowledge
15. Archaic
    a) of, or pertaining to, arches
    b) pertaining to archangels
    c) retention or imitation of what is old or obsolete
    d) a former variation of the word archery
    e) of or pertaining to rainbows
16. Kinetic
    a) relating to the movies, or moving pictures

b) related to cattle, or kine
c) producing or causing motion
d) related to touching
e) related to the science of numbers

17. Ulterior
a) outside the walls of a building
b) beyond the main point, beyond what is evident
c) relating to Ireland
d) painted exterior walls
e) the finest of its kind

18. Plutocracy
a) rule of the wealthy
b) rule of Pluto in the Underworld
c) rule by the smartest
d) rule of the masses
e) rule by the majority

19. Prerogative
a) ruling powers of a state
b) enjoyed by exclusive privilege
c) original laws, prior to amendment
d) newspaper freedom of information
e) payment for special rights

20. Luminescent
a) emitting sounds
b) multicolored lights
c) glittering
d) related to a particular family of plants
e) emitting light other than as a result of incandescence

Time finished ____________

3

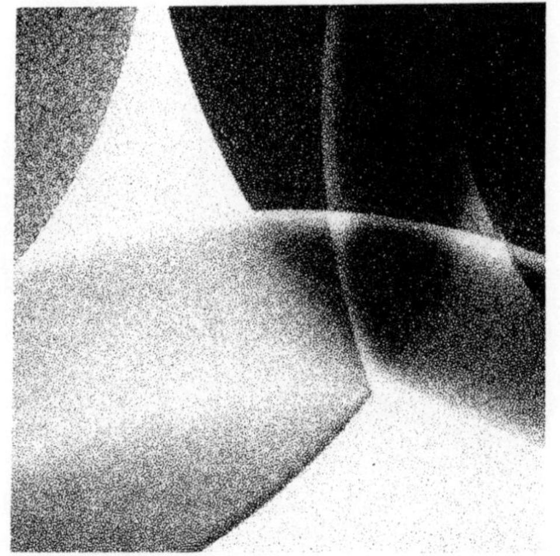

ANALOGIES

Warm-Ups

Instructions for this practice quiz are the same as for the others. Try each of the puzzles, see how well you can do and keep score. After you check your answers, try to find where you went wrong in the ones you missed. When you feel you are ready, try the timed test, which will match you against Mensa members who took the same test.

1. 6 is related to 36 as 4 is related to:
   a) 8 b) 16 c) 24 d) 44 e) 34
2. Stalactites are to stalagmites as ceiling is to:
   a) roof b) floor c) windows d) cave
3. A square is to a cube as a circle is to a:
   a) pyramid b) cone c) sphere d) octagon
4. Books are to libraries as weapons are to:
   a) tents b) guns c) soldiers d) armories
5. A medal is to bravery as wages are to:
   a) money b) work c) hours d) unions

6. Star is to rats as reward is to:
   a) mice b) ransom c) drawer d) fame
7. A rainbow is to the East as the Aurora Borealis is to:
   a) Northern Lights b) South c) North
   d) color
8.

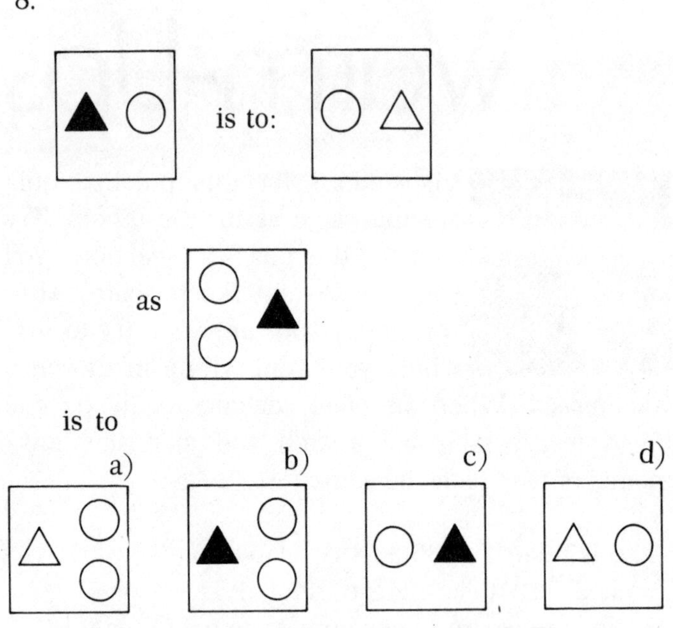

9. Clouds are to rain as springs are to:
   a) river b) summer c) weather d) boats
10. £ is to England as ¥ is to:
   a) France b) Japan c) Yemen d) Australia
11. Wimbledon is to tennis as Pebble Beach is to:
   a) swimming b) golf c) sailing d) running

12. Gutenburg is to printing as Mercator is to:
    a) books b) chemistry c) maps d) astronomy
13. Silver is to metal as oats is to:
    a) grain b) horses c) cake d) food
14. A well is to a cellar as a cave is to a:
    a) hill b) basement c) valley d) river
15. Skin is to people as carapace is to:
    a) lions b) cats c) shellfish d) birds
16. Solar is to sun as terrestrial is to:
    a) moon b) stars c) earth d) planets
17. GRAIDAM is to DIAGRAM as DOLENG is to:
    a) LENGTH b) GOLDEN c) GLADDEN d) OLDING
18. The Leaning Tower is to Pisa as the Tower Bridge is to:
    a) New York b) London c) Edinburgh
    d) Paris
19. Zeus is to Jupiter as Hermes is to:
    a) Cupid b) Hercules c) Mercury d) Venus
20. Daimler is to automobiles as Hughes is to:
    a) motorcycles b) airplanes c) gliders
    d) motorboats

Analyzing Analogies

An analogy is a comparison of things that are somewhat alike. A camera is analogous to the human eye. A computer is analogous to the human brain. An education is analagous to a set of tools.

All too often, *education* is mistaken for *intelligence.* "He must be pretty smart; look at all the degrees he has." Unfortunately, nothing could be further from the truth. Education is simply the acquisition of information and an indication of the ability to make such acquisitions. It would be relatively easy for me to acquire a first-rate set of woodworking tools, but that wouldn't make me a good carpenter. Whether you are an artist does not depend on how many paints, brushes, canvases, and easels you can acquire. To be a good carpenter, I must first have carpentry skills. To be an artist, you must first have talent.

An education is precisely analagous. A skilled carpenter can construct marvelous devices with a good set of tools, just as a talented painter can create masterpieces with the right appurtenances. But give the carpentry tools to the artist and the paints to the carpenter, and, unless either or both happen to be twice blessed, the results are likely to be discouraging. In the same way, if you give a quantity of facts or information to a dimwit, you will have an educated dimwit, who is likely to ignore—or, worse, misuse—the tools. If you doubt that, take a minute or two and search your memory. If you are over twenty-one, you will more than likely recall a teacher, a physician, a lawyer, a clergyman, a boss, a psychologist, or any other member of a highly-educated calling for whom the word "dummy" is almost a kindness.

One of the elements in that nebulous, indefinable quality we call "intelligence" is the ability to relate things—objects, people, events, circumstances—to other things. The facts—the tools one uses—have an effect on the job one does, but the *way* those tools are used have a much greater effect. A really good carpenter who understands how things relate to each other can do a respectable job with the tools and materials on hand, but a klutz will botch the job, no matter how well-equipped his workshop.

What has all this to do with analogy quizzes? This type of quiz tests two factors: To some extent, it tests your general store of knowledge, your toolkit. More important, however, it tests your ability to see how things relate to each other, how ideas can connect. If you know you can do that, you can begin seeking relationships, connections, in all sorts of circumstances. For example, if, as mentioned earlier, the camera is analogous to the human eye, then the reverse must be true. Perhaps, then, the basic principles of cameras could be adapted to replace a human eye that has failed. It should come as no surprise to you that the technology for doing just that exists and that experimenters and researchers are very near the full development of artificial "eyes" that serve more than cosmetic purposes.

When we asked Mensans to tell us how they improve and develop their own intelligence, we did so in an open-ended manner, without specifying categories as such. It is interesting, therefore, that several responses, while not addressing the specific topic of analogies, nevertheless alluded to analogical thinking and attitudes. My favorite reply is from E. W. Paulson, of Rosebury, Oregon. Mr. Paulson's letter was handwritten on a yellow legal pad. Across the first page is a pencilled outline of a left hand. "I know you said typed, double-spaced, 8½ × 11, white . . . the pencil mark around my hand explains why I can't type. . . ." Indeed it does. I have never met Mr. Paulson and know nothing about him (other than the fact that he is a Mensan, and the information given in his letter), but it is reasonable to assume that he suffers from swollen hands, making typing quite impossible. Analogies, you see, are an important first step to deductive reasoning. But back to Mr. Paulson's letter:

> The fourth grade was the best of my twelve years in school. After about three weeks of putting up with my deviltry because I had lots of time to think of things, the teacher got me by the ear and sat me down by one of the other kids with strict orders to spend my time helping him. Ralph wasn't dumb; he was just slow to catch on. The challenge of getting him to understand was fun. In the process of explaining or trying different approaches to the problems, I learned a great deal more about [the] subject myself. My deportment went from undesirable to exemplary, and Ralph's grades [changed] from D's and F's to B's and C's. For me, school changed from a bore to a fun challenge and Ralph changed from hating school to almost liking it. That little Swedish girl who put me to work to keep me out of her hair is now, more than fifty years later, my favorite of all the teachers I had.
>
> I find, yet today, that if I have to explain something to someone who finds it hard to understand, I have a better view or grasp of the concept when I have tried several approaches so the other person can understand. I get more than I give. In trying to put things together to make a picture for someone else I get a clearer one for myself.

It must be a source of considerable satisfaction to E. W. Paulson to know that for half a century he has been able to use his ability to show how things relate to each other, and how those relationships in turn relate to individuals, all the while helping others *and* developing his own awareness of the world around him.

Let's get back to those tools. No matter how skilled you may be, it's almost impossible to do any job without tools—the more tools and the higher their quality, the better the result. Thus, in order to be really adept at visualizing relationships—i.e., analogies—one should attempt to acquire tools. Betty C. Dillingham, of Houston, disclaims any tricks or devices. "To keep my mind in shape," she says, "I simply exercise my curiosity. Frequently, regularly, and unstintingly." She is, by her own admission, "addicted to the printed word. . . . In addition to reading," she continues, "I observe everything my eyes behold or other senses reveal. Having made an observation . . . curiosity is aroused, and I'm off on another mind-stretching adventure, major or minor."

The concept of teaching, explaining, and even learning by analogy seems to be commonplace in the intelligent mind, so much so that it is often used without much premeditation. Jean Hopkins Jackson, a Los Angeles Mensan, wrote to describe a mind-improving technique that, while interesting, I am reluctant to recommend because I believe it requires a skill that at best is difficult to acquire, and, I suspect, is probably inherent. Despite the typical childhood admonitions about doing homework while listening to television (or, depending upon one's age, the radio), Jean can, in fact, read and listen to her radio at the same time. Not only that, but "in a classroom, I now [simultaneously] read textbooks and listen to the lecturer." (She did not explain, and I dared not ask, how she takes notes.) How does she do it? To describe the process, she uses an analogy, albeit one that she is not at home with. "I seem to be able to juggle both tracks; something, I guess, like both tracks on a tape recorder, although I am not too familiar with that technology."

Familiar or not, what could be clearer?

Now, see how well you can do with analogies. As we've pointed out more than once, these quizzes are intended mostly for fun. Still, developing the ability to see analogies, and acquiring the information with which to do so, could significantly change how you work, think, and relate to people. Practice. It's worth it.

Match Wits with Mensa

ANALOGIES TEST

Time started ___________
Time elapsed ___________

Choose the word or number in the second pair that is most closely related to the first. For example: Apple is to pear as veal is to a) pork b) fish. The answer would be a, since apple and pear are both fruit and veal and pork are both meat.

1. Potatoes are to peanuts as apples are to:
   a) bananas b) lilies c) peaches d) tomatoes e) cucumbers
2. Spain is to Argentina as Portugal is to:
   a) Trinidad b) Brazil c) Mexico d) Guyana e) Canada
3. Celsius is to 0° as Fahrenheit is to:
   a) 100° b) 0° c) 32° d) 212° e) 112°

4. Drachma is to Greece as peseta is to:
   a) Mexico b) Italy c) Canada d) Brazil
   e) Spain
5. Loops is to spool as straw is to:
   a) pinker b) hay c) painting d) warts
   e) rosy
6. Napoleon is to Melba as macadam is to:
   a) roads b) poinsettia c) overshoes d) trees
   e) food
7. Rich is to money as leafy is to:
   a) vase b) foliage c) mountain d) flower
   e) dog
8. The number 2 is to 8 as 5 is to:
   a) 15 b) 100 c) 125 d) 10 e) 60
9. 1789 is to France as 1649 is to:
   a) Germany b) Switzerland c) New Zealand
   d) United States e) England
10. The letter A is to E as B is to:
    a) C b) D c) G d) H e) Q
11. Retort is to chemist as ramekin is to:
    a) painter b) engineer c) dressmaker d) cook
    e) lawyer
12. Black Beauty is to horse as Lassie is to:
    a) cow b) bird c) dog d) whale e) camel
13. Palette is to artist as kiln is to:
    a) potter b) painter c) goldsmith d) writer
    e) cook
14. Ceylon is to Sri Lanka as Constantinople is to:
    a) New Constantine b) Leningrad c) New
    York d) London e) Istanbul

15. *The Raven* is to Poe as *Gone With The Wind* is to:
    a) Mitchell b) Keats c) Robbins d) Susann
    e) Blake
16. Star is to constellation as constellation is to:
    a) sun b) earth c) galaxy d) planetoid
    e) moon
17. Onions are to leeks as crocuses are to:
    a) apples b) saffron c) tulips d) lilacs
    e) bananas
18. Reagan is to Carter as Truman is to:
    a) Dewey b) Jackson c) Kennedy d) Roosevelt e) Johnson
19. Halley is to comet as Broca is to:
    a) printing b) tires c) automobiles d) brain
    e) fruit
20. ◠ □ △ / ● ◠ ★ is to ★ ◠ ● / △ □ ◠

    as ◠ ■ ● / ★ ● ○

    is to:

    a) ● △ ▲ / ◠ ● ★ b) ○ ● ★ / ● ■ ◠ c) ◠ ■ ▲ / ★ ☆ △ d) ○ ○ ▲ / △ △ ◠ e) ▲ ● ○ / ◠ △ ●

Time finished ___________

4 MATHEMATICS,

REASONING, & LOGIC

Warm-Ups

1. Five men raced their cars on a racing strip. There were no ties. Will did not come in first. John was neither first nor last. Joe came in one place after Will. James was not second. Walt was two places below James. In what order did the men finish?
2. A soldier has been captured by the enemy. He has been so brave that they offer to let him choose how he wants to be killed. They tell him, "If you tell a lie, you will be shot, and if you tell the truth, you will be hanged." He can make only one statement. He makes the statement and goes free. What did he say?
3. You go shopping with $60. You spend 1/4 on clothes, $30 for equipment for your home computer, and 10 percent of your original money on some food. How much do you have left?

4. If Sally's daughter is my son's mother, what relationship am I to Sally if I am male?
5. In the following series of numbers, fill in the missing number: 35, 28, 21, ____
6. By following the same rules used for the signpost, how far is it to Moscow?

7. A cup and saucer together weigh twelve ounces. The cup weighs twice as much as the saucer. How much does the saucer weigh?
8. What figure should come next in the following series?

9. Paul usually beats Patty at croquet, but loses to Joe. Tom wins most of the time against Patty, and sometimes against Paul, but cannot beat Joe. Who is probably the worst player?
10. A rule has been followed to make each of the sample words in parentheses. The words in parentheses are related to the words in both the first and last columns. Using the same method, fill in the missing word.

tend	(teal)	also
evert	(even)	enter
late	(______)	stone

11. You are working in a store where they have been very careless with the stock. Three boxes of socks are incorrectly labeled. The labels say Red Socks, Green Socks, and Red and Green Socks. How can you relabel them correctly by taking only one sock out of one box?
12. Following the same rule that has been used to place the following numbers, add the next two numbers in their proper places:

1			4			7
	2	3		5	6	

13. Joe has red hair. Some people with red hair have terrible tempers. Therefore, Joe has a terrible temper. True, false, or uncertain?
14. Your friend has invented a new variety of paper-and-pencil game, like tic-tac-toe, but three in a row *loses*. Below is the diagram of a game. You are o and it is your turn. What move must you make? (Remember: Three in a row loses.)

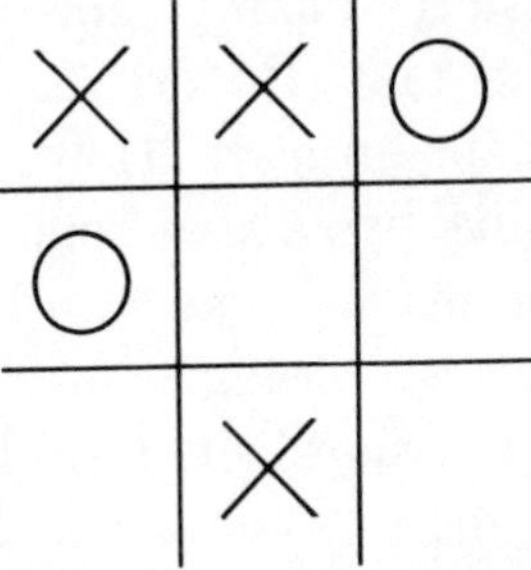

15. What two numbers come next in the following series?
    1 6 2 7 3 8 ? ?

16. A woman collects antique snuff boxes. She bought two, but found herself short of money and had to sell them quickly. She sold them for $600 each. On one she made 20 percent and on the other she lost 20 percent. Did she make or lose money on the whole deal? And how much?
17. A forty-foot length of chain, of uniform weight per unit of length, hangs between two buildings, attached at the same height at both ends. The shape of this chain is called a "catenary." If the distance from the points of suspension to the lowest point of the chain is twenty feet, how far apart are the buildings?
18. There are four seats in a row at a concert. Philip will sit next to Sally, but not next to Gerald. If Gerald will not sit next to John, who is sitting next to John?
19. A man hires a taxi to meet him at the railroad station at 3 p.m. to take him to an appointment. He catches an earlier train and arrives at 2. He decides to start walking, and is picked up en route by the taxi. He arrives twenty minutes early for his appointment. How long did he walk?
20. A woman buys two dozen apples and one dozen oranges. She makes a pie with half of the apples and squeezes six oranges for juice. Next time she goes to the store, she buys half as many apples and oranges as she has left. How many pieces of fruit does she then have altogether?

BONUS:

The Mensa diet, which follows, was invented by Jerry Salny at an air force base during World War II, while trying to cool off and lose weight at the same time. It has been printed in numerous Mensa publications and in another quiz book, which said it could not be solved. It can.

The Mensa Diet

Everybody knows that losing weight is a matter of burning up more calories than are taken in. Everyone also knows that a calorie is that amount of heat required to raise the temperature of one gram of water (pure water, under standard conditions) by one Celsius degree.

Let us take a glass of scotch and soda filled with ice. Assuming that this is 200 grams (200 cc), and neglecting the fact that scotch can lower the freezing point, and overlooking the bubbles in the soda, the temperature must be 0° Celsius, since the glass contains melting ice.

Drink the scotch and soda.

Somehow, the body must supply enough heat to raise the 200 grams to body temperature, or 37°C. The body must supply 200 grams × 37°C or 7,400 calories. Since all the calorie books show scotch as having 100 Calories per ounce, and none at all for the soda, we should be able to drink scotch and soda all day and lose weight like mad.

This has been tried, and although the experimenter hasn't lost any weight in the process, he doesn't worry about it much anymore. Why doesn't it work?

Adding It Up

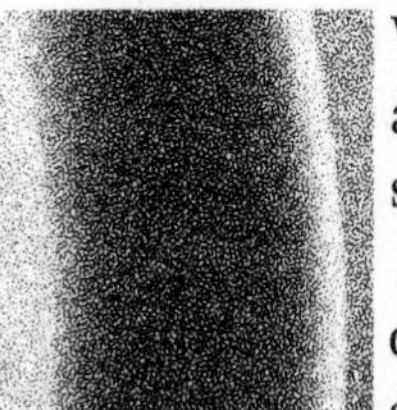

Why lump mathematics, reasoning, and logic questions together in a single group?

When that question was put to our test maven, Dr. Abbie Salny, she replied, "Many people don't like to be confronted with a lot of math questions at one time. They get bored. Some even become intimidated." Of course, there are many people who love math problems, but they seem to be a minority. Also a minority, but nevertheless present, are those who simply hate math, primarily because they can't seem to get it right. If math were the only criterion for the IQ score that qualifies for Mensa membership, I wouldn't even have tried to make it; I consider it an exceptional day when I can get my checkbook to balance on the second try. (I am, perhaps, one of the few people who actually was entitled to a tax refund after an Internal Revenue Service income tax audit;

I had made a serious error in adding up my gross income. Gross.)

There is another good reason for grouping mathematics, reasoning, and logic together: If you consider it for a moment, you'll see that it's reasonable and logical—it all adds up.

There's no arguing with mathematics. There can be only one right answer. To be sure, there is often considerable argument as to how to arrive at that answer, which is why people highly skilled in math often come up with different answers to the same problem. The more complex the problem, the likelier it is that there will be more than one right answer. Wait a minute—didn't I just say that in mathematics, there can be only one right answer? That's where reasoning and logic come in. If you know your stuff, you'll follow the mathematical steps, in logical order, to arrive at a solution.

Frequently, such logical processes are somewhat abstract, perfectly applicable in "pure" math, but something less than practical in real life. If you're confronted with a problem that begins "Assume you are travelling at the speed of light," you don't have to be a mathematician to realize that you're dealing with an exercise in mental gymnastics and not something you're likely to come across in your daily routine. So it is sometimes necessary to attack a problem from the standpoint of what is logical, and then examine it in terms of what is reasonable. Life, alas, is not always logical. (It is in these quizzes, however, so there's no need to worry about that, at least for now.)

It can be fun and profitable to massage the mind with self-imposed math problems. Brenda Evans Hart discovered, some years back, "that amid the hustle and insanity of Houston traffic, if I didn't figure out a way to calm myself and develop patience, I would either die of a heart attack or ram the nearest car." She began by tuning in the local classical-music station and found that "the metronome-like beat [of the music] had a calming effect on my nerves." An interesting observation: Have you ever noticed the close relationship between music and mathematics—half- and quarter-notes, the numerical designations of tempo (a waltz is played in 3/4 time), the numerical divisions of sections of music (eight bars to the measure), etc.? Brenda soon found that while the music calmed her, she needed something to occupy her more-tranquil mind, so she began devising math problems relevant to her surroundings. "If I live twenty miles from work," she writes, "and take two hours to get home, having stopped on the freeway forty-five times, what is my average speed . . . and can I walk it faster?" This, she claims, had an additional soothing effect. "Before I knew it, I was home, out of traffic, and feeling fine.

"I took this addictive serenity from my car into my home," she wrote, "and found myself working old college-text calculus problems to the sounds of Bach whenever I found life getting to be too much." (To each his own: I'll keep the Bach and swap the calculus problems for a book of British crossword puzzles, thank you.) Brenda moved her mental gymnastics into the office ("My boss thought I was very busy and was, therefore, pleased"), and then added to them by playing a variation of the "Dictionary" game (described in the Vocabulary section). That, in turn, led to a love affair with the English language and a desire to improve her use of it.

While she heartily recommends these methods of improving one's own intelligence, she includes two cautionary notes: First, she insists that it must be a continuous effort, on the premise that, as with some other activities (such as sex), if you don't use it you'll lose it. Second, she is a staunch advocate of physical fitness. Nevertheless, she insists that her techniques work, at least for her. "If the ability to make a high score on a test is an indication of being smart," Brenda Evans Hart writes, "then, yes, I am smarter today than I was a few years ago because a few years ago, my test scores would not have gotten me into Mensa. I attribute this to a sharpening of my analytical skills in an attempt to cope with insanity and boredom with mental order and physical good health." She signed her letter, "Sincerely," and I believe her.

In any argument or debate, the winner usually has reasoning and logic on his or her side (although they are all too frequently overshadowed by emotion and prejudice). Nancy Reller, of Kent, Ohio, has developed a technique that sharpens her own thinking and arms her with reasoning and logic when the situation calls for it. Her inspiration also struck in the midst of traffic. "On the way to work one morning," she relates, "I was listening to a discussion [on the radio] on whether eighteen-year-olds should have the vote. The announcer asked listeners to call in with their opinions and I decided to call as soon as I got to work, since it was a subject on which I had strong feelings. That was when it hit me that I didn't really know exactly what my opinion was, much less being able to put it clearly and in a few words."

The realization shocked her, because she felt that the subject was one in which she was well versed. It is also a sign of her intelligence—at least in my opinion—that she was able to face the fact that she didn't know. "Forgetting the phone call," she continues, "I started putting down on paper everything I could think of on the subject, important or not." In a one-woman brainstorming session, she discovered that what at first had seemed unimportant took on new prominence. She studied her list, selected what she considered "the best of the facts," arranged them in a logical and reasonable sequence, "and from that composed a paragraph. This was studied in turn, and the whole thing rewritten, several times. Finally, I could say, 'This—briefly—is my opinion.' " And I guess that it would be difficult to argue against it.

Using mathematical precision, logic, and reasoning, however, seems to be the province of those with orderly minds. What resources are available to those of us whose thoughts—and even deeds—seem to be scattered all over the place? Since logic and reasoning appear to have been missing from the package handed me at birth, I have had to find adequate substitutes. My own method should win me a certificate of appreciation from the people who manufacture index cards. When I have to put together an article or a book, I do all my research, including taped interviews, and then carefully review everything, extracting facts or other useful bits of data—impressions, quotes, "color," etc. Each bit of data is transferred to a separate index card (not necessarily physically; I often use a simple cross-referencing system). I then begin jotting down, on more cards, those general elements that have to be included in the work. These are done helter-skelter, as they occur, with no attention to detail or order, and each idea earns its own card. I then arrange the idea cards in what strikes me as a logical sequence. I now have a working outline and I simply drop the "fact" cards behind the appropriate idea cards. The next step is to arrange the cards in each section in some sort of sensible sequence, at which point, there's nothing left to do but the writing. It seems to work. How well it works you can judge for yourself: you are holding the product of such an effort in your hands right now.

Richard Hazelett, of Provo, Utah, has found an elaborate variation of this technique to be helpful in increasing his knowledge and intellectual prowess. In an essay (previously unpublished) entitled "How Not to be Scatterbrained—Sometimes," he writes: "In order to improve my mind and also to get things done, I write on a *separate* pocket-sized slip of paper each idea, problem, chore, or citation to search in a library. I keep the problem-slips in my wallet, as Lincoln used to keep them in his stovepipe hat, and then I go over them at odd moments." The idea slips are sorted by projects. "If the object is an article or book," he claims, "it almost writes itself that way," a claim that I can wholeheartedly support. "Chores are sorted according to priority or convenience." Lest one get the impression that Richard's wallet is enormous, he adds that something on the order of a hanging-folder file is extremely useful.

Thus, even if you are not mathematically inclined, and fail to arrange your ideas—or even your life—in a logical way, and tend to let emotions overcome reason, there are ways to compensate.

All you have to do is think logically and reasonably about how to be logical and reasonable.

Match Wits with Mensa

MATHEMATICS, REASONING, AND LOGIC TEST

Time started ____________

Time elapsed ____________

1. A man goes to visit his friend thirty miles away. He doesn't mind speeding, so he travels at 60 miles per hour and arrives in half an hour. On the way back, however, he has a little trouble with his car, and it takes him an hour to reach home. What was his average speed for the round trip?
2. You are in a country where there are only liars and truthtellers, and they cannot be told apart by sight. You set out on a dangerous trip, because there is a fork in the road that can lead either to a crocodile swamp or to safety. When you reach the fork, the signpost is gone, but there are two

men standing there. You know that they will answer only one question between them. What question can you ask either of them that will tell you which road is safe?

3. A horse salesman went to a horse auction with a certain number of horses. To his first customer, he sold half his horses, plus half a horse. To his second, he sold half of what he had left, plus half a horse. To the last, he sold half of what he had left, plus half a horse. Each of his customers received whole horses, however, not half horses, and he had no horses left. How many horses did he start out with?
4. 0 1 2 3 4 5 6 7 8 9 = 1
   Put the appropriate plus or minus signs between the numbers, in the correct places, so that the sum total will equal 1.
5. A man went into a jewelry store and bought a $75 chain, giving the clerk a $100 bill. He returned a few moments later and bought a new catch, giving the clerk a $20 bill and receiving $5 in change. Later, the bank told the store that both the $100 bill and the $20 bill were counterfeit. Ignoring markup, overhead, cost of merchandise, etc., how much money did the store lose?
6. You are playing a new game of tossing cubes with numbers on them. The numbers are given below. The winner is the one who first reaches 100, using the fewest numbers possible, and no

repeats. Which numbers do you need?
5 17 19 37 41 46 50 66

7. Robert and Rose went shopping for presents together. They had a total of $264 between them. Rose had $24 more to begin with but she spent twice as much as Robert and ended up with two-thirds as much money as Robert. How much did Robert spend?
8. Next week I am going to have lunch with my friend, visit the new art gallery, go to the Social Security office, and have my teeth checked at the dentist's. My friend cannot meet me on Wednesday, the Social Security office is closed weekends; the art gallery is closed Tuesday, Thursday, and weekends; and the dentist has office hours only on Tuesday, Friday, and Saturday. What day can I do everything I have planned?
9. If a jet has a value of 1, and a plane has a value of 2, what is the value of a Concorde?
10. Complete the series by adding the next number:
0 0 1 2 2 4 3 6 4
11. Multiply by 6 the number of 9's followed by 2, but not followed by 7, in the number below:
92563123979864134928929596
12. X is less than Y; Y is not equal to Z. Therefore the statement that: X is not equal to Z, is:
a) correct b) incorrect c) undetermined.
13. A man bets $24 and gets back his original bet and $48 additional. He spends 25 percent of his winnings at a restaurant to celebrate, and 50 per-

cent of his winnings to buy a present for his wife because he was so late, and his salary was $240, from which he made his original bet. How much money does he lave left when he finally arrives home?

14. What is the next number in the following series:
    – 2 4 –12 48 –240 ____
15. You are at a meeting at which there are only liars and truthtellers. A woman comes up to you and says that the chairman of the meeting told her he was a liar. Is she a liar or a truthteller, and how do you know?
16. Three youngsters on our street went shopping for clothes in a very unusual clothing store. The owner charges $3 for a tie, $3 for a hat, and $5 for a shirt. How much would a jacket cost?
17. How many minutes is it before six o'clock if fifty minutes ago it was four times as many minutes past three o'clock?
18. A man just finished painting his house and needs something more. At the hardware store the clerk shows him what he wants and says, "one is $1.". "Fine,"says the man,"I took 600, so here's $3." What had he bought?
19. How many odd pages are there in a book 479 pages long?
20. What is the missing number in the following sequence?
    3 7 15 ____ 63 127

Time finished ____________

5

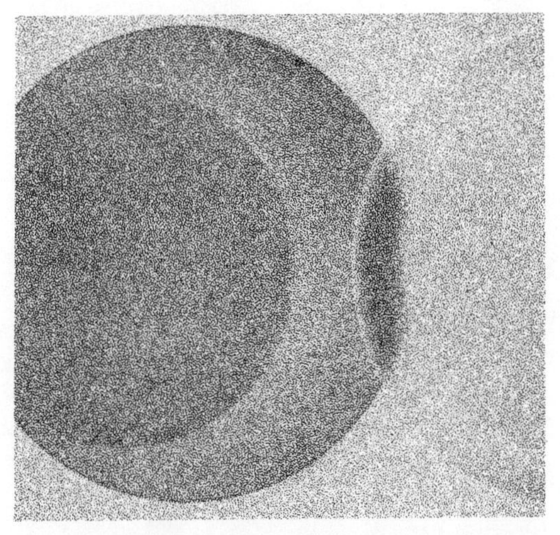

CLASSICS

Warm-Ups

1. If a teenager and a half can eat a pizza and a half in a day and a half, how many pizzas can a dozen teenagers eat in three days?
2. How far can a dog run into the woods?
3. Which is heavier, a pound of gold or a pound of feathers?
4. In a strange town, there are only two barbers. Looking into the barber shops, you see that one barber is messy and disorganized, and has a terrible haircut. The other barber is neat and tidy, and has a beautiful haircut. Which one do you pick to cut your hair, and why?
5. Sally comes to school one day, and for Show and Tell announces to her kindergarten class that today is the birthday of both her father and her grandfather, and what is more, both are exactly

the same age. Her teacher tells her that is impossible, but Sally insists that she is right. Can she be?

6. If you have black socks and brown socks in your drawer, mixed in the ratio of 4 to 5, how many socks will you have to take out to make sure of having a pair the same color?
7. Six thousand, six hundred six dollars is written \$6,606. Now write eleven thousand, eleven hundred eleven as fast as you can.
8. There is a low railroad trestle in your town. One day you see a large truck stopped just before the underpass. When you ask what's happened, the driver tells you that his truck is one inch higher than the indicated height of the opening. This is the only road to his destination. What can he do to get through the underpass the easiest way?
9. Even if you never had a word of Latin, you should be able to read and understand the following poem:

   O sibili si emgo.
   Fortibuses i naro.
   O nobili demis trux.
   Vatis inem? Caus an dux.

10. I have two coins that add up to 55¢. One of them is not a nickel. What are the two coins?
11. Punctuate the following sentence so that it makes sense:
    Jim where Bill had had had had had had had had had was right.
12. On your bookshelf you have three books in a set,

Volumes I, II, and III. Unfortunately, you also have a book worm who is eating up your books. The books are each two inches thick, and the covers are each a half inch thick. If the hungry bookworm starts at the outside front cover of Volume I and eats through to the last page of Volume III before you find him, how many inches of book material has he eaten?

13. Divide 100 by 1/2 and add 10. What do you have?
14. You have just tossed a coin that has come up heads for the tenth time in a row. What is the probability that it will come up heads the next time?
15. A man is stalking a bear that has attacked his camp. He reports later that naturally he went south. What color was the bear?
16. A young explorer called his expedition chief in great excitement to report that he had just found a golden coin marked 6 B.C. The expedition chief fired him. Why?
17. Sam Jones lives on the eighteenth floor of an apartment building. Every morning when he goes to work, he gets on the elevator, presses the ground floor button, and rides down. Every night when he comes home, if he is the only one in the car, he gets off at the sixth floor and walks up the rest of the way. He would prefer to ride. Why does he walk?
18. John wants to win a club election very badly, but there are two other candidates and all have re-

ceived an equal number of votes. They decide to settle the election by pulling the winning name out of a hat. John writes one opponent's name on the top part of a sheet of paper, his own in the middle, and the other opponent's name on the bottom. Then he tears them apart, places the strips in the hat, and offers to draw out a name. How does he make sure he wins, even though he is adequately blindfolded?

19. A poor but honest knight wants to marry a beautiful princess, and she wants to marry him. The king offers the knight a choice. He can draw one of two slips of paper from a golden box. One will say "Marriage," the other "Death." The princess manages to whisper to her suitor that both slips say "Death." But the knight and the beautiful princess are wed. How did he accomplish this?
20. One store in town is selling a small radio for $20. Its rival is advertising the same radio on sale for only one thousand, nine hundred ninety-nine pennies. How much will you save by buying it on sale?

Classic Conundrums

If some of the practice questions you've just gone through seem familiar, it's because they've been around for ages. Many of them are tests of knowledge, logic, and reasoning ability. And many of them are so-called "trick" questions. The relationship of trick questions to intelligence is worth looking at a little more closely.

In the not-too-distant past, the expression "native American intelligence" was commonplace. These days, however, it seems to have lapsed into disuse. Why? Has native American intelligence ceased to exist? Have we, as a nation, lost our ability to think? Probably not. I admit that mine is a personal and untested theory, but I believe that over the years, we have been culturally conditioned to abandon thinking as unnecessary. Everything—news, information, entertainment, medical care, food, merchandise—is provided in neat packages, predigested, preconditioned: Just add water, batteries not included. We've lost the habit of thinking for ourselves.

Intelligence implies the ability to think, and an IQ score implies the existence, to a greater or lesser degree, of intelligence. But that IQ score is an index of a potential. Whether the size of that potential is variable or expandable within a given individual is the subject of considerable debate. The extent to which that potential is used, however, is not debatable: Either you use it or you don't. With the best of intentions, it is difficult to use if it is confined by boundaries.

If you've come this far in the book, then you probably have a fair idea of your own potential by now. If you think you have a high IQ, you are making a mistake if you believe that alone is enough to qualify you as "intelligent." If, on the other hand, your scores are lower than you would have liked, you are making a mistake if you believe there is nothing you can do about your intelligence. It has been said before, but it bears repeating: Use it or lose it.

You don't need any teachers, counselors, psychologists, or gurus to help you expand your intelligence. All you need is the desire to do so and the initiative to practice. Ask questions. Understand everything, even if it has to be explained several times or in a new way. Give free rein to your curiosity. Most important of all, free yourself of those mental boundaries I mentioned earlier.

That brings us back to those trick questions. What makes them tricky is that they rely on the likelihood that your thinking is conditioned to move in only one direction with respect to the information given. When you are given the answer, you feel a little foolish, perhaps even irritated, because you've been taken advantage of. That's because you instantly realize that you should have known the answer all the time, if only you'd thought about it. But you couldn't have thought about it because your thinking process was preconditioned.

Farfetched? Melodramatic? Try it yourself on relatives or friends, with these old chestnuts. First, set them up—precondition their thought processes; then zap them with the right answers and see what happens. Begin with the "Scottish Names" gambit. (This should be done orally; it's too easy to solve when seen in print.) Ask your victim to pronounce M-A-C-T-A-V-I-S-H. After he or she has done so, try M-A-C-C-A-R-T-H-Y; then M-A-C-D-O-U-G-A-L. You can use any other "Mac" names, as long as they are legitimate. After each name has been pronounced in turn, ask the sucker to pronounce M-A-C-H-I-N-E-S. As you can see, that spells *machines,* but if your victim doesn't answer with "MacHines," it's safe to assume that he or she has fallen into the trap before. By spelling out the "Mac" names first, you will have effectively preconditioned the listener's thinking, leading it straight down a predetermined—and totally incorrect—path. Talk about tricky.

Here's another one that is better spoken than written. How do you pronounce:

C H O
P H O
U S E ?

Again, you're setting your victim up by placing the letters in groups of three (as I have attempted to do by arranging them in a square), again preconditioning thinking. As a result, you're likely to get an answer approximating something like "Show - foe - use." What kind of a word is that? No kind, of course. Did you fall into the trap? Did you allow me to dictate your thought processes, or were you able to break through the boundaries and simply string the letters out in a row to arrive at *chophouse*? (Not many young people may be familiar with that word to begin with. Never mind; this gambit works almost as well with *flophouse*.)

One more supposedly trick question, this one to demonstrate how it isn't even necessary for you to set the person up; you can simply take advantage of the preconditioning that already exists. Punctuate the following: TIME FLIES I CANT THEYRE TOO FAST. Most people will stick in the missing apostrophes immediately, but then they're stymied. Look how simple it is, once you free up your thinking (the quotation marks are a little added refinement to aid comprehension): "Time flies." "I can't. They're too fast." Still doesn't make sense? Look again. The problem is that you're already familiar with the cliche, "Time flies." In that expression, *time* is a noun and *flies* is a verb, and your conditioning leads you to assume that it has to be that way. It doesn't. Read the punctuated sentence again, but this time consider *time* as the verb and *flies* as the noun. Tricky? Only if you insist on retaining the strictures placed on your mind, on your native intelligence.

If you think these mental somersaults are of little value in the real world, try paying closer attention, say, to television commercials. When the announcer tells you that a particular brand of toilet paper has more sheets per roll than the leading competitor, he is telling the truth. The assumption is that *you* will assume—because it's implied, although not actually stated—that all toilet paper sheets are the same size. But if you compare brands in the supermarket, you may find that in fact, the total quantity is exactly the same, because although one brand has more sheets, the individual sheets are smaller.

There are other benefits to opening your mind, to attempting to see familiar things in new ways. There are several names for what results—imagination, creativity, insight, even intelligence.

The sermon being preached here is a simple one: Whatever role heredity may play in intelligence, environment plays at least as important a role. The only way to improve, enhance, and develop your intelligence is first, to decide to do it, and then, to do it.

Most Mensa members apparently agree. Vicky Edwards Gehrt is a freelance journalist who lives in Villa Park, Illinois. She conducted an informal survey among her fellow Mensans to use as the basis for an article she's working on and prepared a short summary for this book. Here is her report:

In a survey I conducted with 327 members of Mensa, I asked participants to describe the major environmental factors they considered responsible for their intelligence. The responses provide a guideline for those who wish to assure themselves that they are not letting their potential go to waste.

The foremost consideration was reading. Many respondents noted that their parents read to them when they were children. Parents were also influential by providing reading materials in the home, by encouraging the use of the public library, and by setting an example by their own reading habits.

Intelligent people tend to be heavy readers throughout life. They read for information and entertainment. Although the reading habit should ideally be established during childhood, it is possible to develop a love for reading at any age. . . . Intelligence needs to be nourished with a steady supply of newspapers, magazines, and books.

Several participants also mention personal drive as a factor in intelligence. They believe that the desire to learn is vital, and take every opportunity to fulfill that desire. When they encounter a new concept, they find out more about it; when they discover a new area of interest, they delve into it wholeheartedly; and when they have questions, they find answers.

Other considerations in the development of intelligence noted by participants include the following:

Playing word games and doing word puzzles; playing strategy games; limited television viewing; enrichment activities (lessons, education courses); cultural activities (concerts, theater, museums); travel; hobbies, collecting, pursuit of personal interests; contact and conversation with intelligent people.

That seems to sum things up nicely, especially the part about contact and conversation with intelligent people. If that appeals to you, consider joining Mensa. You'll find the address in the back of this book. But first things first.

Match Wits with Mensa

CLASSICS TEST

Time started ____________
Time elapsed ____________

This is a collection of many of the old time puzzles and "foolers" that you have read and heard for many years, in one form or another. How many do you remember? If you don't remember them, can you figure them out?

1. A man wants to grow a tree very quickly. He buys some special tree seeds that double in height every day. On the tenth day, the tree is twenty feet high. On what day was it five feet high?
2. A snail is climbing out of a well. The well is twenty feet deep. Every day the snail climbs up three feet and every night he slips back two feet.

How many days will it take him to get out of the well?

3. A man moors his boat in a harbor at high tide. A ladder is fastened to the boat, with three rungs showing. The rungs are twelve inches apart. At low tide the water level sinks twenty feet. How many rungs of the ladder are now showing?
4. If there are twelve one-cent stamps in a dozen, how many two-cent stamps are there in a dozen?
5. A child is injured in an accident and rushed to the hospital. The doctor takes one look at the child and says: "I can't treat him, that's my son." The doctor is not the child's father. How do you explain this?
6. There is a family party consisting of two fathers, two mothers, one grandfather, one grandmother, two sons, and one grandson. Only five people are there. How is this possible?
7. You are very tired and go to bed at 8 P.M. However, you have a very important appointment at 10 A.M. the next day and don't want to oversleep, so you wind up your alarm clock and set it for 9. How many hours do you sleep?
8. Your doctor gives you six pills and tells you to take one every half hour. How long does it take you to use up all of the pills?
9. How many months have twenty-eight days?
10. How many pairs of animals did Moses take on the Ark?
11. What is the next letter in this series? O T T F F S S E N ?

12. You have two pencils, a good one and a cheap one. The good one cost $1.00 more than the cheap one. You spent $1.10 for both. How much did the cheap one cost?
13. You are cutting a board twelve feet long into one-foot pieces. How many cuts must you make? (Stacking the pieces is not allowed.)
14. A fly is flying between two boys on bicycles who are pedalling toward each other at 10 miles per hour. The fly reaches one boy, reverses immediately, and flies back to the other boy instantly, repeating the process each time. The fly is flying at 60 miles per hour. The boys meet in thirty minutes. How far has the fly flown in that time?
15. You are driving alone on a dark night, and pass through Dogpatch (you can see its name on the City Hall). About half an hour later, you reach a five-way crossroads, but the sign has been uprooted and is lying in such a position you cannot tell exactly how it stood. How do you find out which of the roads leads to Crosspatch, your destination? (You are not allowed to invent a convenient passerby).
16. In thirty seconds or less, give the number that is double one half of 99,637,543,667,345.
17. A very fast train runs from A to B in an hour and a quarter, but on the return trip it takes 75 minutes under identical conditions. Why?
18. What word, when you add additional letters, becomes smaller?
19. Does Canada have a 4th of July?

20. Under international law, if a plane crashes in the middle of the Atlantic, where would the survivors be buried?

Time Finished ____________

ANSWERS

TRIVIA WARM-UP ANSWERS

1. El Greco, the painter.
2. Hungary.
3. Phileas Fogg (and his valet, of course).
4. Wine.
5. Australia.
6. George Orwell; all three are pen names, but the other two are female.
7. They are both tidal islands, cut off from the mainland at certain tides, and a chapel sits on each.
8. Off the coast of Newfoundland, Canada; they belong to France.
9. Butcher, baker, and candlestick maker.
10. The Richter Scale.
11. Trees; there are living sequoias that are believed to be several thousand years old.
12. **Alaska—also the westernmost; the 180th parallel runs through it, so it is both.**
13. Brasilia.
14. From Captain Boycott, a land agent in Ireland who was ostracized for refusing to reduce rents.
15. At Lake Success, in New York.
16. Your wife.
17. Probably not; a lycanthrope is a werewolf.
18. Feast of St. Stephen.
19. Tanganyika
20. Ursa Major.
21. Aphrodite.

22. For engineering canals: Suez and Panama.
23. Canada and the United States, on the west coast.
24. 7 A.M.
25. In southern New Jersey.

TRIVIA TEST ANSWERS

Listed after each of the following answers is a percentage figure that represents the percentage of Mensa members taking this quiz who answered correctly. Give yourself one point for each correct answer. If you answer a question that fewer than 15 percent of Mensa members answered, give yourself double credit for that answer.

The average number of right answers obtained by Mensa members was twelve. The average time taken was seven minutes.

1. Voltaire. (33%)
2. Francisco Pizarro. (55%)
3. Sweet white wine. (33%)
4. In London, England. (41%) (One member answered: "In a communist plot.")
5. Finland. (10%)
6. They are basically wingless; they can't fly. (48%) (Incidentally, the kiwi is *not* extinct.)
7. A three-panel painting. (55%)
8. Cellini, who was a sculptor, not a painter. (37%)
9. Pain, which is measured in dols. (17%)

10. The number 13. (72%)
11. Henry VIII; she was Catherine of Aragon, his first wife. (52%)
12. Mark Twain. (93%)
13. Styx. (85%)
14. Portugal; however, Lusitania also included some of Spain. (10%)
15. Alben W. Barkley, Harry S Truman's vice president (v.p. = "veep"). (31%)
16. Dynamite, or explosives. (83%)
17. Guernsey, Jersey, Alderney, Sark, and Herm—any two. (31%)
18. Ceylon. (12%)
19. Archery. (72%)
20. Heraldry. (86%)
21. Spinach. (50%)
22. Pt. (33%)
23. Generally southeast. (59%)
24. Denmark, although it was recently granted home rule in many areas of legislation. (55%)
25. On Staten Island, New York, having crossed from Bayonne, New Jersey. (14%)

VOCABULARY WARM-UP ANSWERS

1. c) His intelligence, as measured, was *paramount*.
2. d) The explorer photographed the *pagans'* religious rituals.

3. c) The doctor's explanation *allayed* the woman's fears.
4. d) The girl assumed the pose of a *suppliant* before her tormentor.
5. c) Many emperors hope to found a *dynastic* line.
6. b) *Feudal* laws were very exact on the duties and obligations of lords and vassals.
7. b) The actor *improvised* his speech when his co-star forgot her lines.
8. b) The movie studio put the mousy aspiring actress through a veritable *metamorphosis*; now she looks like Jean Harlow.
9. a) The spoiled child went into a *paroxysm* of anger when he was refused a new toy.
10. d) You could never be sure of her actions, since she usually behaved in a *capricious* manner.
11. d) The king said the entertainment presented to him was unsatisfactory because it was too *plebian*.
12. c) The crusading newspaper referred to the gambling casino as a "den of *iniquity*."
13. b) The man who suddenly acquired a great deal of money built a *pretentious* home in the Country Club section.
14. b) Mensa is now *extant* in dozens of countries in the world.
15. d) The woman was greatly *perturbed* when she lost her purse.
16. c) The traitorous Duke was arrested for trying to *usurp* the throne.

17. c) Hamlet saw an *apparition,* the ghost of his father.
18. d) My former teacher, who was an expert in *circumlocution,* could take a paragraph just to say, "Hello."
19. a) The new congressman found a *staunch* ally in the senior representative from his own state.
20. b) People do not wish to live in areas where there are *noisome* vapors.

VOCABULARY TEST ANSWERS

Again, the numbers in brackets after each answer show the percentage of Mensa members who gave the correct answers.

The average Mensa member who took this test got eighteen right. The average time taken was five minutes. Twenty-two percent of the Mensa members who took this test received perfect scores.

1. c) There was a *conglomeration* of objects on the cluttered table. (96%)
2. c) Economic *stagnation* is usually undesirable for a country. (100%)
3. b) *Eloquent* speech is not always accompanied by wisdom. (96%)
4. d) A snake makes a *sibilant* sound. (75%)

5. b) Many anecdotes told about famous people are probably *apocryphal.* (56%)
6. c) He was *inveigled* into an illegal card game by the clever gambler. (85%)
7. a) The reasons for the murder were the usual *sordid* ones. (100%)
8. b) *Antagonism* between nations is often deep-rooted. (100%)
9. c) Many alleged cures for disease are promoted by *mountebanks.* (88%)
10. c) A good stage magician is usually skilled in *legerdemain.* (96%)
11. a) The competency of many people is *implicit,* until they demonstrate otherwise. (96%)
12. d) Having one state far more powerful than the others in an alliance usually results in *hegemony.* (70%)
13. a) The surveyors walked the *periphery* of the area they were working on. (96%)
14. b) The mother was very *solicitous* of her sick child. (88%)
15. c) The word *thou* is often considered an *archaic* usage. (100%)
16. c) Ballet is considered a *kinetic* art. (100%)
17. b) There is sometimes an *ulterior* motive behind seemingly simple actions. (93%)
18. a) *Plutocracy* is derived from the Greek words for *wealth* and *rule.* (78%)
19. b) Each branch of the American government has certain *prerogative* powers not enjoyed by the other branches. (93%)

20. e) Fireflies are *luminescent*. (96%)

ANALOGIES WARM-UP ANSWERS

1. b) 16, the number 4 squared.
2. b) Floor—top and bottom.
3. c) Sphere; three- and two-dimensional.
4. d) Armories, where weapons are stored.
5. b) Work; a reward for effort in each case.
6. c) Drawer—the word reversed.
7. c) North; locations are given.
8. a) Reversed and missing color.
9. a) River; in each analogy, the second word represents the source of the first.
10. b) Japan—the sign is for the Japanese yen.
11. b) Golf.
12. c) Maps.
13. a) Grain.
14. c) Valley—the second analogy pairs natural hollows or holes; the first pairs man-made ones.
15. c) Shellfish.
16. c) Earth.
17. b) GOLDEN—an anagram.
18. b) London.
19. c) Mercury; Zeus and Hermes are Greek names of gods; Jupiter and Mercury are the Roman forms.
20. b) Airplanes.

ANALOGIES TEST ANSWERS

The percentage after each question shows the percentage of Mensa members who got that question correct. No one received a perfect score. The average score was fifteen correct. The average time was just over ten minutes. (The highest score, nineteen correct, was accomplished in three minutes!)

1. c) Both grow on trees as potatoes and peanuts both grow underground. (71%)
2. b) Both of the second pair speak Portuguese, as both of the first pair speak Spanish. (86%)
3. c) 32° is freezing on the Fahrenheit scale, as 0° is freezing on the Celsius scale. (86%)
4. e) Pesetas are the monetary unit in Spain, as drachmas are in Greece. (34%)
5. d) Each is the reverse of the word. (67%)
6. b) The first pair are names of people applied to food; macadam and poinsettia are the names of people applied to objects. (10%)
7. b) Foliage refers to leaves. (87%)
8. c) The number cubed: 2 × 2 × 2 equals 8; 5 × 5 × 5 equals 125. (81%)
9. e) The year when a revolution took place. (33%)
10. a) The first pair is the first two vowels, the second is the first two consonants. (20%)
11. d) A ramekin is a small baking dish. (57%)
12. c) Both are famous animals of their kind. (81%)
13. a) Potter. (95%)

14. e) Istanbul is the new name of Constantinople, as Sri Lanka is the new name of Ceylon. (80%)
15. a) Margaret Mitchell wrote *Gone With The Wind.* (80%)
16. c) Each is part of a larger grouping. (89%)
17. b) They are members of the same family. (14%)
18. d) Carter preceded Reagan and Roosevelt preceded Truman, as U.S. president. (71%)
19. d) Both were scientists who studied astronomy and the human brain, respectively. (67%)
20. b) Top and bottom lines reversed, right to left reversed. (89%)

MATH, REASONING, AND LOGIC WARM-UP ANSWERS

1. James was first, followed by John, Walt, Will, and Joe.
2. He said, "I will be shot." If he were shot, it would be the truth, and if they hanged him it would be a lie. So they set him free.
3. $9.00; do one step at a time.
4. Sally's son-in-law.
5. 14; it is the 7 × multiplication table backwards.
6. 10 miles—5 miles per vowel in the word.
7. 4 ounces, or 1/3 of the total weight.

8. The second white figure, reversed; the pattern starts with three black stars interspersed with white figures, and then it begins again with the same figures reversed.
9. Patty, because all of the others usually either beat her or beat somebody else who beats her.
10. Last; the first two letters of the first word and first two letters of the last word are used.
11. Take a sock out of the box labeled Red and Green. You know all the boxes are mislabeled, so the box labeled Red and Green *cannot* contain two colors. If the sock is green, put the green label on that box, and switch the other two labels; if the sock is red, attach the red label and then switch.
12. 8 and 9, both of them below the line. Numbers with curved lines go below the line; straight lines go above.
13. Uncertain; it says "some," which means others don't.
14. Put your 0 in the lower left-hand corner, then he cannot avoid losing.
15. 4 and 9. There are actually two series. The first starts with 1 and continues in sequence in every other place. The second starts with 6 and follows the same procedure.
16. She lost money. From the facts given, one cost her $500 and the other $750. So she paid $1250 for them and then sold them for $1200, losing $50 in the process.
17. The buildings are together. Draw a diagram. If

you missed this one, don't feel bad. A young physicist who later won the Nobel Prize worked it out at 60 feet, using a mathematical formula for a catenary.

18. Philip. They would sit in this order: John, Philip, Sally, Gerald.
19. He walked 50 minutes; the taxi saved 10 minutes going and 10 minutes coming back.
20. Twenty-seven apples and oranges.

BONUS: There are *gram* calories and *kilo* Calories, the first spelled with a small c and the second with a capital C, and a kilo Calorie is 1,000 times greater than the other. One ounce of scotch contains 100 kilo Calories, so you take in 100,000 calories and use up only 7,400, and continue to gain weight.

MATHEMATICS, REASONING, AND LOGIC TEST ANSWERS

The number in parentheses after each answer is the percentage of Mensa members who answered that question correctly. The average number of correct answers was twelve. The average time was twenty-seven minutes.

1. 40 miles per hour. (This is deceptive. You do not add up the time and divide by two. You figure that he traveled sixty miles—there and back—in

ninety minutes, or an hour and a half. That gives you the right answer.) (65%)

2. You ask either man: "Which road would the other man tell me was safe?" and take the opposite. If you ask the liar, he will tell you the unsafe road, because the truthteller would have pointed out the right road. If you ask the truthteller, he will tell you the truth, that the liar would have named the unsafe road. In either instance, whomever you ask will point out the unsafe road. So you take the other one. (25%)
3. Seven. The first man gets three-and-a-half, plus one-half, or four horses. The second man gets half of the three that are left, one-and-one-half, plus one-half, making two. That leaves one, so the last man gets one-half and one-half. If you start from the end and work backwards, it's easier. (45%)
4. $0+1+2-3-4+5+6-7-8+9 = 1$
   There are probably other solutions. If you check your answer and it is correct, give yourself full credit. (55%)
5. $120—the two counterfeit bills. (55%)
6. 17, 37, 46. (80%)
7. $48. (35%)
8. Friday; just cross out days that can't be used. (80%)
9. 3—one for each vowel. (25%)
10. 8. There are two series of numbers, both starting with zero. The first is 0, 1, 2, 3, 4, in every other place. The second is 0, 2, 4, 6, 8. (20%)

11. Three 9's meet the requirements; multiplied by 6, the answer is 18. (50%)
12. c. (90%)
13. $252. (60%)
14. 1440. The first number in the series is multiplied by negative 2, the second by negative 3, the third by negative 4, and so on. (70%)
15. She is a liar. No liar would claim to be a liar, therefore she is not telling the truth. (55%)
16. $6. The storekeeper charges $1 per letter in the name of the item. (35%)
17. Twenty-six minutes. (35%)
18. His house number. (30%)
19. 240. (85%)
20. 31. Double each number and add 1 to get the next number. (85%)

CLASSICS WARM-UP ANSWERS

1. Twenty-four. One teenager can eat one pizza in a day and a half, or two pizzas in three days.
2. Only half-way; after that, the dog is running *out* of the woods.
3. A pound of feathers is heavier, because it weighs 16 ounces. Metal is weighed in troy ounces, of which there are 12 to the pound.
4. Get your hair cut by the sloppy barber. He's the one who gave the neat barber his beautiful haircut.

5. Of course. For example, her father could be 50, and her mother's father (her grandfather) is also 50. (Her mother is much younger than her father, obviously.)
6. Only three. If you take out three socks, you are guaranteed a pair.
7. 12,111.
8. Let enough air out of the tires to lower the truck.
9. Oh, see Billy, see them go.
   Forty buses in a row.
   Oh, no, Billy, them is trucks.
   What is in them? Cows and ducks.
10. One of them *is* a nickel: a 50¢ piece and a 5¢ piece.
11. Jim, where Bill had had, "had," had had, "had had." "Had had" was right.
12. Three and a half inches. Put a set of books on the shelf and look at them. If the worm started at the *front* cover of Volume I and ate through Volume II, he would not have touched the pages of Volume I at all. Volume II, with cover, would be three inches, and the worm would eat only the cover of Volume III, another half-inch.
13. 210. If you divide a number by 1/2, you double it.
14. The chance it will come up heads is 1 in 2. A coin has no memory.
15. White. He was at the North Pole if he could only go south and the bear was a polar bear.
16. There is no way in which a genuine coin could be marked B.C. B.C. means Before Christ, and

certainly no coins were minted indicating an era marked by someone who had not yet been born.

17. He's a midget and can't reach the button for the eighteenth floor.
18. He feels for the two torn edges of the paper with his name on it.
19. The poor but honest and clever knight tears up the paper he picks, and offers the other one to the king. Since the untorn one says "Death," obviously, says the knight, the one he tore up said "Marriage."
20. You save 1¢: That is $19.99.

CLASSICS TEST ANSWERS

Each of the answers is followed by an indication of percentage. That is the percent of Mensa members who got that particular question right. The average number of correct answers was seventeen. The average elapsed time was fourteen minutes. Of all the Mensa members who took this quiz, only 6 percent got perfect scores.

1. The eighth day. If it doubles each day, on the ninth day it was ten feet high, on the eighth day it was five feet high. (84%)
2. Eighteen days. On the eighteenth day he reaches the twenty-foot level and climbs out; he doesn't have to fall back. (56%)

3. The number of rungs showing will be the same, as long as the boat is afloat. (94%)
4. Twelve, just as there are in any dozen. (98%)
5. The doctor is a woman, and the child's mother. (94%)
6. Grandfather, grandmother, son, daughter-in-law, and grandson. The grandfather and son are both fathers, the grandmother and daughter-in-law are both mothers, and the son and grandson are both sons. (91%)
7. One hour. On a wind-up alarm, it will ring at 9, which is one hour after you set it. (97%)
8. Two and one half hours. (97%)
9. Every month has twenty-eight days; most of them also have more. (94%)
10. Noah, not Moses. (95%)
11. T, for Ten. The sequence is *O*ne, *T*wo, *T*hree, etc. (84%)
12. Five cents. The expensive one was $1.05. If you thought the answer was $1.00 and 10¢, that does not meet the requirements. $1.00 is not $1.00 more than 10¢, it is 90¢ more. (84%)
13. Eleven cuts. (91%)
14. The fly flies thirty miles. None of the information is important except that the fly flies at 60 miles per hour and he flies for half an hour. The fly therefore flies thirty miles. (71%)
15. Pick up the signpost, point the sign to Dogpatch back the way you came, and all of the other signs will also point the right way. (53%)

16. 99,637,543,667,345. If you take one half of any number and double it, you have the number you started with. (91%)
17. One hour and a quarter is 75 minutes; there is no difference. (84%)
18. Small. (87%). (There were some clever answers here, like *meter* and *millimeter*. If you thought up one like that, give yourself credit.)
19. Yes, it comes between the third of July and the fifth of July, but it isn't a holiday for Canadians. (91%)
20. Nowhere. You don't bury survivors. (69%)

A Word about IQ and What It Is and Is Not

There is probably no psychological concept more used and abused than IQ. A very brief history will indicate why this is so.

Close to 100 years ago, Alfred Binet devised a series of tests to help the French government select children for classes for the retarded. He set up a series of tests, found out what ages they matched, and devised a scale based on this. If a four-year-old, for example, passed the four-year tests, he had an Intelligence Quotient of 100. This was obtained by dividing his Mental Age (M.A.) by his chronological age (C.A.). Because it was calculated MA/CA= (moving the decimal point two places to the right), the result was called a quotient.

This plan worked for a good many years, but it was obvious, even from the beginning, that there were many problems. A three-year-old, for example, who passes the six-year tests, and would thus have an IQ of 200, really cannot do what a six-year-old can. And when you reach the upper teens, the results cannot be computed this way. Why? Because it is difficult to measure intellectual growth in adulthood. Most people seem to reach a plateau in reasoning and many other processes. (Some claim it occurs at 13 or 14, which is why you often hear that certain films, books, etc. are geared to the average 13-year-old: That is a misinterpretation of this very fact.)

Rationally, you can't compare an 18-year-old and a 36-year-old on this sort of scale, so testers came up with another concept: Deviation IQ. This simply means that you—your wits, knowledge, intelligence—are matched against others in your own age group. If you're a 70-year-old, for example, you are matched against others over 65, and not with 30-year-olds. You are marked on a relative standing in your own group.

So what do IQ's mean? Nothing in themselves. As a relative measure, Intelligence Quotient is no longer an accurate description, but a rusty, misleading cliché. Your "percentile rank" is the more preferred score. A percentile rank means "the number below": For example, the percentile rank required for Mensa is the 98th. That means that ninety-eight out of every hundred people would score lower on the particular type of test taken.

But even here one important caution is in order: Even the concept of intelligence and how to measure it, is under severe criticism right now. Does pure intelligence exist? And if so, do intelligence tests measure it fairly?

Long-term studies of several hundred children—identified as "genius level" about 50 years ago—indicate that scoring well on an IQ test does predict school success. The children, now older adults, who have been studied continuously, achieved academic successes far above expectancy. They also tended to be far above average in most other measures as well, physical health, and financial success among them. However, not all of these high scorers did equally well. The reason is clear. An IQ test does not measure drive, persistence, creativity, or any of the myriad other skills that often count for more in achieving success out of school. A low score on an IQ test does not mean probable failure in life. All it means is that the person taking the test did poorly on that particular test. Most of us do not spend our lives in situations that can be measured by paper and pencil tests. Since this is so, scores obtained on such tests should be viewed with some restraint if they are very high and with some scepticism if they are low. They measure only one aspect of a total life pattern.

Mensa Mini Test

Just how smart are you? Have some fun with this Mensa Mini-Test. You can check answers with the key on page 142.

1. is to as is to

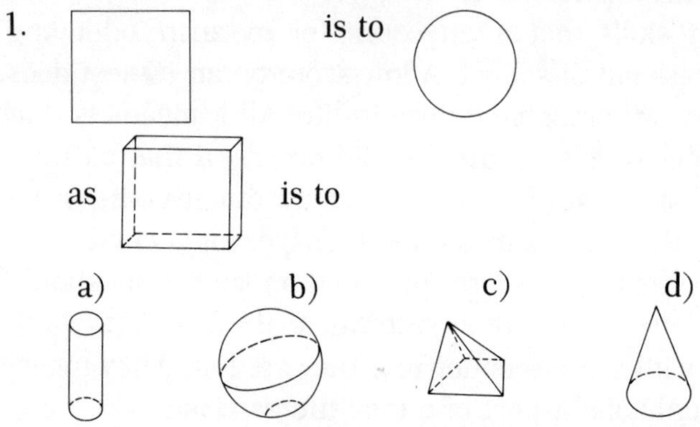

2. The arrows represent a simple code. What word(s) could they spell when rearranged?

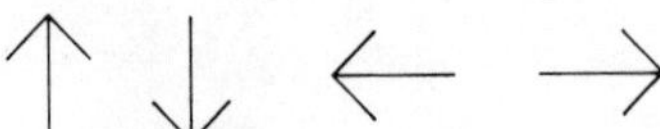

3. Given the statement, "You'd <u>better</u> solve the problem or <u>I'll</u> solve it for you!", pick out the relationship most likely to be represented.
   a) Doctor to patient
   b) Examiner to test taker
   c) Father to son
   d) Lawyer to client
4. Find a word meaning the same as the left hand

word in one sense and the right hand word in another sense.

hard ______________ company

5. If $M \times E = 6$; $N \times S = 20$; $E \times S = 15$; $E \times N = 12$; $S \times A = 30$; then $M \times E \times N \times S \times A = ?$
6. Alex, Allan, Carol, Celia and Sharon took intelligence tests. Celia scored higher than Carol, Allan scored higher than Celia, and Carol outscored Alex. Sharon scored lower than Allan. Therefore:
   a) Celia scored higher than Alex but lower than Carol
   b) Both Alex and Allan outscored Celia
   c) Celia outscored Alex by more than she outscored Carol
   d) Sharon scored higher than Carol
   e) None of the above
7. Which one of these would usually not belong?

   design, equation, paragraph, poem
8. 3 is to 9 and 18, as 2 is to 8 and?
9. All Mensans who reside in New Hope have become members by taking a supervised intelligence test. The barber in New Hope qualified for Mensa through a school achievement test score.
   a) The barber should be required to take a supervised test to qualify.
   b) The barber does not live in New Hope.
   c) The barber was unable to take the supervised test when it was given.
   d) The barber formerly lived in New Hope and then moved out.
10. Which bottom figure belongs with the top figures?

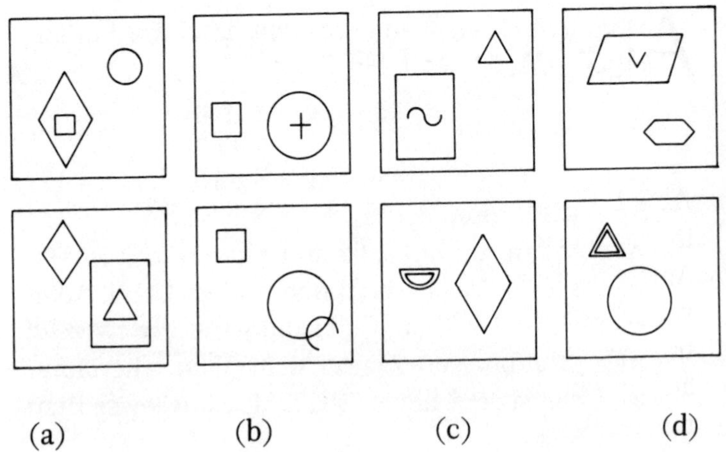

Key

(1) b (2) News, Sewn, Wens (3) c (4) firm (5) 720
(6) c (7) design (8) 24 (9) b (10) a

Have you answered at least six questions correctly? If so you've done fairly well! Drop us a line if you'd like to know more about us. Include $8.00 check or money order and we'll send you a standard I.Q. test that you can take in the privacy of your own home.

About The Authors

ABBIE F. SALNY, Ed. D., is a psychologist licensed in the State of New Jersey, and a diplomate of the American Board of Professional Psychology. In private practice, she specializes in supervising doctoral trainees (i.e., people who have received their doctorates but need practical experience) and in diagnostic testing.

She is a retired professor and deputy chairman of the psychology department at Montclair (NJ) State College. A Mensa member since 1964, she serves as supervisory psychologist for both American Mensa and International Mensa. Her husband, Jerome E. Salny, a retired business executive, is also a Mensa member. That's where they met.

MARVIN GROSSWIRTH is a journalist and author whose books and articles cover a wide variety of subjects, with a propensity for science, technology, and medicine. He joined Mensa in 1961 and has served as the organization's public relations officer continuously for twelve years, except for a two-year term as national chairman. He is married to Marilyn S. Grosswirth, a technical writer, whom he met at a Mensa party. They both read a lot to their son, Adam.

How To Join Mensa

If you'd like to join Mensa, you can find out how by writing to Mensa, Dept. AW, Brooklyn, NY 11223. In Canada, write to Mensa, P.O. Box 505, Station S, Toronto, Ontario, Canada M5M 4L8. You'll need a score on an IQ test that's at the 98th percentile or higher. Mensa can help you take such a test. If you've already been tested, they'll tell you how to submit "prior evidence."